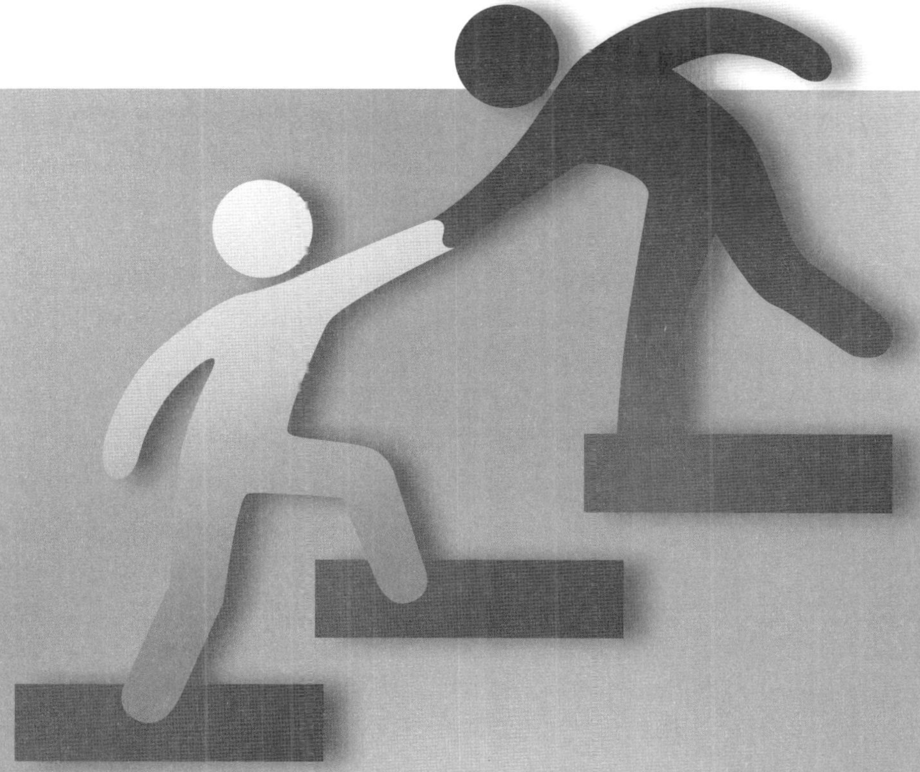

MANAGING UNSTOPPABLE LEARNING

TOM HIERCK

Edited by Douglas Fisher and Nancy Frey

Solution Tree | Press

Copyright © 2019 by Solution Tree Press

Materials appearing here are copyrighted. With one exception, all rights are reserved. Readers may reproduce only those pages marked "Reproducible." Otherwise, no part of this book may be reproduced or transmitted in any form or by any means (electronic, photocopying, recording, or otherwise) without prior written permission of the publisher.

555 North Morton Street
Bloomington, IN 47404
800.733.6786 (toll free) / 812.336.7700
FAX: 812.336.7790

email: info@SolutionTree.com
SolutionTree.com

Visit **go.SolutionTree.com/behavior** to download the free reproducibles in this book.

Printed in the United States of America

Library of Congress Cataloging-in-Publication Data

Names: Hierck, Tom, 1960- author. | Fisher, Douglas, 1965- editor. | Frey, Nancy, 1959- editor.
Title: Managing unstoppable learning / Tom Hierck ; editors, Douglas Fisher and Nancy Frey.
Description: Bloomington, IN : Solution Tree Press, [2019] | Includes bibliographical references and index.
Identifiers: LCCN 2018012996 | ISBN 9781945349881 (perfect bound)
Subjects: LCSH: Professional learning communities. | Curriculum planning. | Educational planning. | Teachers--Professional relationships. | Teacher-principal relationships.
Classification: LCC LB1731 .H5135 2019 | DDC 371.1/06--dc23 LC record available at https://lccn.loc.gov/2018012996

Solution Tree

Jeffrey C. Jones, CEO
Edmund M. Ackerman, President

Solution Tree Press

President and Publisher: Douglas M. Rife
Editorial Director: Sarah Payne-Mills
Art Director: Rian Anderson
Managing Production Editor: Kendra Slayton
Senior Production Editor: Tara Perkins
Senior Editor: Amy Rubenstein
Copy Editor: Jessi Finn
Proofreader: Evie Madsen
Text and Cover Designer: Laura Cox
Editorial Assistant: Sarah Ludwig

This book is dedicated to the educators and learners in Woodridge, Illinois. School District 68 is making gains in student outcomes, and the educators there have demonstrated a willingness to continue to grow and learn to improve those outcomes. I have learned a lot during my five years of association with the schools there, and it has helped shape my thinking as I continue to work in schools and districts in other jurisdictions. I am indebted for the opportunities the district provided and the knowledge I gained. I hope this book does some justice to your efforts.

As with every undertaking of this magnitude, time must be taken from somewhere. More often than not, it also means others must pick up some responsibilities. Thanks to my wife, Ingrid, I am able to create books like this and assist colleagues in their professional learning and growth. I have said it far too often for it to be believed anymore, but there will be a last book project soon, and more time returned to our lives. Your support is immeasurable and deeply appreciated

Acknowledgments

It is always an honor to have your name appear on a book cover, and the thrill of seeing each one does not fade. Having said that, none of the books I've authored would be possible without the incredible support of the team whose names do not appear on the front cover, so let me share them here.

The members of the Solution Tree family have been great supporters of my work over time, and we are nearing double digits of titles in the Solution Tree catalogue with my name on them. Thanks to Douglas Rife for his never-ending encouragement; Claudia Wheatley for her indefatigable support; Jeff Jones for building a company for educators driven by educators; Shannon Ritz and the professional development team for getting the work out to colleagues via events; Erica Dooley-Dorocke and the marketing team for promoting the work in various formats; and the editorial efforts of Tara Perkins, who pushed me hard to make the book even better.

Trusted colleagues are often the backbone of any successful writing endeavor. A huge thanks goes out to some excellent ones who have been working in Woodridge, Illinois, for many years and who opened their schools to me five years ago as we developed a very powerful connection. Patrick Broncato is the superintendent and provides leadership that allows schools to thrive. Greg Wolcott is the assistant superintendent for teaching and learning, and has devoted his professional career to making a difference for students and colleagues. His fingerprints are evident throughout this text. William Schmidt is the assistant superintendent for human resources, and formerly led the junior high school that I feature in this book. I value the hours of conversation we had as he helped to shape the success of the school. Justin Warnke is the new principal of Thomas Jefferson Junior High School and was previously the assistant principal. He has a great understanding of behavior, the needs of students, and the skill sets adults need to create positive outcomes. He spent numerous hours with me shaping the narrative that appears in the appendix of this book, and I am indebted to him for that assistance and appreciative of all that he taught me.

Additional colleagues who provided insights include my good friend Chris Weber, who is passionate about ensuring behavior does not become the obstacle to student learning. We can talk for hours about the topic, and I always leave energized. Charlie Coleman and I have been on the same wavelength as far as taking a positive approach to behavior management for decades now, starting with our original training on positive behavior intervention and supports. Whenever I got stuck or needed a sounding board, he was able and willing to assist.

Finally, I am once again appreciative of the opportunity to write another book built on the high-quality work of Douglas Fisher and Nancy Frey. They are colleagues and friends who challenge my thinking while also providing insights into improving schools for all learners and educators. The Unstoppable Learning model breaks new ground with the clarity provided around each of the seven elements Fisher and Frey detail. To author a book that focuses on one of the elements was both daunting and enjoyable, and I thank them for their time and support as I crafted this work.

Solution Tree Press would like to thank the following reviewers:

Loreen Flanary
Teacher Specialist Preschool
Logan City School District
Logan, Utah

Tara O'Hea
Special Education Teacher
Hickory Creek Middle School
Frankfort, Illinois

Abby Sandlin
Third-Grade Teacher
Pitner Elementary School
Acworth, Georgia

Sarah Starr
Principal
Longview School
Germantown, Maryland

Shannon Stone
Goal Clarity Coach
Johnsontown Road Elementary School
Louisville, Kentucky

Shondra Walker
Grades 6–12 Principal
Wonderful College Prep Academy
Delano, California

Visit **go.SolutionTree.com/behavior** to download the free reproducibles in this book.

Table of Contents

Reproducible pages are in italics.

About the Editors ix
About the Author xi
Foreword xiii
    By Douglas Fisher and Nancy Frey
Introduction 1
    Systems Thinking 2
    About This Book 6

1 Improving Behavior Management Through Cultural Change 9
    Understanding Culture and Structure 11
    Making a Collective Commitment to the Cultural Change 13
    Assessing Your Current Reality 16
    Aligning the Classroom Culture 16
    The Takeaways 18
    Practices That Promote Positive Outcomes *19*

2 Supporting Teacher-Student Relationships 21
    Expectations, Not Rules 22
    Strategies for Improving Teacher-Student Relationships 25
    The Takeaways 29

3 Supporting Group Interactions and Peer Relationships 31
    Benefits of Group Work 32
    Cautions About Group Work 34
    Behavior and Groups 35
    Strategies for Peer Relationship Support 36
    The Takeaways 42

4 Supporting a Positive Learning Environment 45
Positivity by Design 46
Positivity Outcomes 47
Research-Based Best Practice 48
The Learning Pit 49
Strategies and Tools for Fostering Positive Behaviors 51
The Takeaways 61
The ABC Direct-Observation Tool 62
CICO Form 63

5 Responding to Problem Behaviors 65
The Why of Behavior 66
Educators' Responsibility 66
Academic and Social Behavior Priority Standards 67
Defiance 69
Responses to Defiance 70
Intervention: When and If 75
The Takeaways 78

Epilogue 79

Appendix: A Case Study—Thomas Jefferson Junior High School 81
Background 82
First Year of Behavioral Management Implementation 84
Second Year of Behavioral Management Implementation 87
Third Year of Behavioral Management Implementation 89
Fourth Year of Behavioral Management Implementation 91
Sixth Year of Behavioral Management Implementation 94
The Work Ahead 95
The Takeaways 96

References and Resources 99

Index 105

About the Editors

Douglas Fisher, PhD, is a professor of educational leadership at San Diego State University and a teacher leader at Health Sciences High and Middle College. He teaches courses in instructional improvement and formative assessment. As a classroom teacher, Fisher focuses on English language arts instruction. He was director of professional development for the City Heights Educational Collaborative and also taught English at Hoover High School.

Fisher received an International Reading Association Celebrate Literacy Award for his work on literacy leadership. For his work as codirector of the City Heights Professional Development Schools, Fisher received the Christa McAuliffe Award. He was corecipient of the Farmer Award for excellence in writing from the National Council of Teachers of English (NCTE) as well as the 2014 Exemplary Leader for the Conference on English Leadership, also from the NCTE.

Fisher has written numerous articles on reading and literacy, differentiated instruction, and curriculum design. His books include *Unstoppable Learning, Teaching Students to Read Like Detectives, Checking for Understanding, Better Learning Through Structured Teaching,* and *Rigorous Reading.*

He earned a bachelor's degree in communication, a master's degree in public health, an executive master's degree in business, and a doctoral degree in multicultural education. Fisher completed postdoctoral study at the National Association of State Boards of Education focused on standards-based reforms.

Nancy Frey, PhD, is a professor of educational leadership at San Diego State University. She teaches courses on professional development, systems change, and instructional approaches for supporting students with diverse learning needs. Frey also teaches classes at Health Sciences High and Middle College in San Diego. She is a credentialed special educator, reading specialist, and administrator in California.

Before joining the university faculty, Frey was a public school teacher in Florida. She worked at the state level for the Florida Inclusion Network, helping districts design systems for supporting students with disabilities in general education classrooms.

She is the recipient of the 2008 Early Career Achievement Award from the Literacy Research Association and the Christa McAuliffe Award for excellence in teacher education from the American Association of State Colleges and Universities. She was corecipient of the Farmer Award for excellence in writing from the National Council of Teachers of English for the article "Using Graphic Novels, Anime, and the Internet in an Urban High School."

Frey is coauthor of *Unstoppable Learning*, *Text-Dependent Questions*, *Using Data to Focus Instructional Improvement*, and *Text Complexity: Raising Rigor in Reading*. She has written articles for the *Reading Teacher*, *Journal of Adolescent and Adult Literacy*, *English Journal*, *Voices From the Middle*, *Middle School Journal*, *Remedial and Special Education*, and *Educational Leadership*.

To book Douglas Fisher or Nancy Frey for professional development, contact pd@SolutionTree.com.

About the Author

Tom Hierck has been an educator since 1983 and has held a variety of roles, including teacher, department head, vice principal, principal, director of international programs, sessional university instructor, Ministry of Education project coordinator, and assistant superintendent. This has allowed him the opportunity to see education from a myriad of perspectives that are reflected in his writing.

Hierck is a compelling presenter, infusing his message of hope with strategies culled from the real world. He has presented to schools and districts across North America and overseas with a message of celebration for educators seeking to make a difference in students' lives. Hierck's dynamic presentations explore the importance of being purpose driven in creating positive learning environments and a positive school culture, responding to the behavioral and academic needs of students, and utilizing assessment to improve student learning. His belief that every student is a success story waiting to be told has led him to work with teachers and administrators to create the kinds of learning environments that are effective for all educators while building strong relationships that facilitate learning for all students.

Hierck was a recipient of the Queen's Golden Jubilee Medallion, presented by the premier and lieutenant governor of British Columbia, for being a recognized leader in the field of public education. He earned a bachelor's degree and teacher certification from the University of British Columbia and a master's degree from Gonzaga University.

This is the ninth Solution Tree title bearing Hierck's name, with number ten now being drafted. He contributed to *The Teacher as Assessment Leader* and *The Principal as Assessment Leader*, coauthored the best-selling books *Pyramid of Behavior Interventions: Seven Keys to a Positive Learning Environment* and *Starting a Movement: Building Culture From the Inside Out in Professional Learning Communities*, and coauthored *Uniting Academic and Behavior Interventions: Solving the Skill or Will Dilemma*, *Strategies for Mathematics Instruction and Intervention, 6–8*, and *Assessing Unstoppable*

Learning. His first solo effort, *Seven Keys to a Positive Learning Environment in Your Classroom*, was published in 2016.

To learn more about Tom Hierck's work, visit www.tomhierck.com or follow @thierck on Twitter.

To book Tom Hierck for professional development, contact pd@SolutionTree.com.

Foreword

By Douglas Fisher and Nancy Frey

"Don't smile before winter break."

Do you recall getting that ridiculous piece of advice as a new teacher? We can only shake our heads at how misguided that directive was. Our field has progressed in many ways since we were in our teacher preparation programs so long ago (before the Internet was invented). Members of the teaching profession in the 21st century look for evidence of practice, align to content standards, and collaborate in professional learning communities. Yet when it comes to managing the learning environment, teachers can sometimes retreat to outdated habits. When confronted with an uncooperative student, the old tapes in their heads turn on: "How did my third-grade teacher handle this situation? She sent the student to the principal's office!" And so they repeat what they witnessed twenty or more years ago, even though it is unlikely to yield any long-term positive result.

Tom Hierck reminds us that managing a classroom is fundamentally, and foundationally, about the quality of the relationships between and among adults and students. The climate in the classroom, as Hierck notes, is about "creating the optimal learning environment that allows every student to experience success regardless of his or her current status, approach, baggage, or disposition" (p. 10). Therefore (and rightly so), issues related to problematic and unproductive behaviors are not raised until chapter 5. So much of what constitutes effective management comes from the investments educators proactively make such that students understand the ways of work, how to seek help, and how they learn about themselves through their interactions with others.

Too often, discussions about relationships and management never occur. Thus, a teacher struggling with maintaining positive relationships with students is left alone to figure things out. That breeds isolation and despair on the part of the teacher, who is left to fend for him- or herself. In a short time, those feelings of discouragement foment, and before long, the blame is shifted to students: "It's not me, it's the kids. They're [*fill in the blank with the excuse of your choice*]."

This hands-off approach can result in misaligned schoolwide procedures and processes. In these schools, classrooms function as silos, with educators giving relatively little attention to how the culture and climate of the school seep from the hallways into the classroom. However, educators should view management as a schoolwide investment. In a systems-driven organization, school leaders consider carefully how the climate of the school impacts what teachers are able to do in the learning environment. It isn't a one-way street—there is a reciprocal relationship between classroom and school climate. A problematic relationship between a single teacher and his or her students negatively impacts the entire school. Likewise, when punitive measures to control students drive a school culture, it undermines wise and supportive teachers.

Managing Unstoppable Learning shines a light on the importance of building relationships, investing in a positive culture, and teaching students how to best interact with others. You will find a blend of practical tips and thought-provoking questions that beg for discussion. In fact, we hope you will read this book in the company of colleagues. We imagine you will discover what we have found to be true: people go into teaching to make a positive difference in the lives of students. The impact we have on young people is amplified when we engage with one another in material ways about our practices.

Introduction

While working with a large group of primary teachers at a daylong session on school culture, I asked the kindergarten teachers to share with the group how early in the school year they could detect the difference between a reader and a nonreader. Most responded that the difference was evident within the first week, and the longest anyone suggested was the first month. With that information, I followed up with a question regarding what happens with the reader and the nonreader at the end of kindergarten. The answers were predictable and reflected what generally happens in most jurisdictions—both students are sent on to grade 1 with the hope that the grade 1 teacher can work some magic to close the gap. This practice continues through the subsequent grades with the same hope. Researcher Hedy N. Chang and senior research associate Mariajosé Romero (2008) point out the folly of this action, also noting the link between academic learning and behavioral learning:

> During the early elementary years, children are gaining basic social and academic skills critical to ongoing academic success. Unless students attain these essential skills by third grade, they require extra help to catch up and are at grave risk for eventually dropping out of school. (p. 3)

This is *not* a kindergarten or early years problem; it's a systemic one. Left unchecked, the gap grows, frustration sets in as students enter secondary school, apathy enters the picture, and some students believe that all hope is lost. Also, these students seek other ways that they can seem successful in their peers' eyes, and negative behavior becomes part of their arsenal. Flagrant behaviors, such as calling out or pushing back on reasonable teacher requests, give these students a certain cachet as the class clown. There is a "cool" factor to this behavior their peers often perceive that sets these students apart. Oftentimes what educators perceive as a lack of will to complete a task or attain proficiency is a cover for a lack of skill in the desired outcomes. When students lack these skills, educators must apply behavior management approaches to support the desired student behaviors and create a positive learning environment. *Behavior management* includes any action educators take to enhance the likelihood that students will choose behaviors that are productive and socially acceptable. Teachers must effectively manage their classrooms to establish and sustain a positive culture and learning environment. To respond to unwanted behaviors effectively, it's critical that teachers reflect on what is maintaining a student's challenging behavior. Recognizing that behavior is a form of communication, and that it is difficult to change because it serves a purpose or function for the student, compels educators to work proactively to reinforce the desired behaviors in their classrooms.

Researchers Joy Lesnick, Robert M. Goerge, Cheryl Smithgall, and Julia Gwynne (2010) offer their insight on the importance of getting students on track early:

> Students who are not reading at grade level by third grade begin having difficulty comprehending the written material that is a central part of the educational process in the grades that follow. Meeting increased educational demands becomes more difficult for students who struggle to read. (p. 1)

The authors go on to suggest that third-grade reading level is a significant predictor of eighth-grade reading level and ninth-grade course performance, even after accounting for demographic characteristics (Lesnick et al., 2010). They further state that students who are above grade level for reading in grade 3 graduate from high school and enroll in college at higher rates than students who are at or below grade level in grade 3 (Lesnick et al., 2010). If the goal is reaching the bar (high school graduation and further pursuits driven by a student's passions or interests) or better for every student, educators must work collectively to close the learning gaps and teach appropriate behaviors with an eye toward intervening early. In order for students' learning to become unstoppable, we must address these issues early. This requires a collective commitment to changing an organization's culture.

Systems Thinking

Douglas Fisher and Nancy Frey (2015), authors of *Unstoppable Learning: Seven Essential Elements to Unleash Student Potential*, offer systems thinking as the structure to accomplish this type of undertaking. They explain, "Systems thinking is the ability to see the big picture, observe how the elements within a system influence one another, identify emerging patterns, and act on them in ways that fortify the structures within" (Fisher & Frey, 2015, p. 2).

Fisher and Frey (2015) also remind us, "As part of a systems thinking classroom, teachers know how to respond to problematic behavior to renormalize the classroom and make learning the focus once again" (p. 13). Systems thinking involves seven specific elements and four principles (see figure I.1). The following sections will clarify these major elements and principles that compose systems thinking.

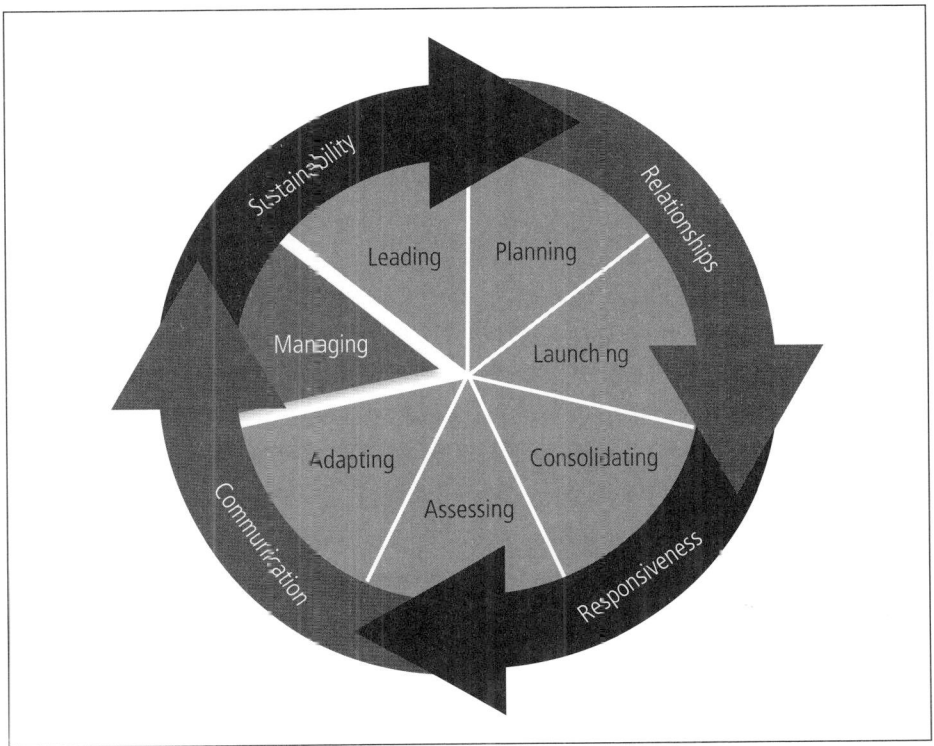

Source: *Fisher & Frey, 2015.*

Figure I.1: Unstoppable Learning components.

Seven Elements of Systems Thinking

Fisher and Frey (2015) identify seven essential elements for both the systems thinking classroom and the systems thinker in order to drive home the importance of (1) planning, (2) launching, (3) consolidating, (4) assessing, (5) adapting, (6) managing, and (7) leading learning in each classroom in a systematic way. All the elements constitute effective practice and are interdependent.

This book will examine the element of managing learning. While the phrasing *managing learning* may sound ominous and conjure up images of control, Fisher and Frey (2015) explain, "That doesn't mean that teachers have to exert tremendous control, exercising their power over students" (p. 13). Managing learning is about setting up the structures that lead to the desired outcomes. It involves achieving consistency as a committed team of educators in order to minimize the impact of negative behaviors and maximize the potential of each student.

Let's make this clear from the outset—we should leave very little about the work in schools to a single individual to address, resolve, or create. In fact, Fisher and Frey (2015) explain, "Every adult in the school has a role in building proactive, healthy relationships with students. These efforts are much more likely to succeed, and quickly, when schoolwide efforts are employed" (p. 151). The growth and development of all students must be the prime objective and the domain of all who interact with those students. My travels as a consultant and author have revealed that educators often find themselves in systems that are not as effective and efficient as they could be. In the absence of a consistent, intentional, and aligned approach—a *we* approach—to creating positive student behaviors, teachers default to a *me* approach, whereby they give their absolute best but rarely achieve consistency—at either the personal or the schoolwide level. However, teachers and principals can establish consistency by using an interdependent approach to managing learning and by recognizing that the end result is the domain of the team, not the individual. Doing so requires *systems thinking*.

Four Principles of Systems Thinking

Fisher and Frey (2015) outline the following four principles that should simultaneously guide educators' work to improve learning systems and ensure unstoppable learning for their students: (1) relationships, (2) communication, (3) responsiveness, and (4) sustainability. It's fair to say that I have encountered many educators whom I would describe as forward thinkers—they employ and nurture these principles daily in their practice—but many work in a system or structure that isn't designed to support them or their efforts to bring these practices into play. As an oft-quoted adage from Albert Einstein suggests, we can't solve today's problems by using the same kind of thinking we used when we created them. If a school's end goal is to improve its current results, then its actions will need to change to achieve that end. Education authors Tom Hierck and Angela Freese (2018) suggest, "This means aligning in unity around a singular focus of *learning* instead of perpetuating the cycles of organizational chaos that cause forward thinkers to become overwhelmed and debilitated in their work" (p. 4). This also reminds me of a scene from one of my favorite Christmas stories, *A Christmas Carol*, where Ebenezer Scrooge suggests, "If the courses be departed from, the ends will change" (Dickens, 1843, p. 115). If we change the inputs, then surely the outputs will also change.

I believe every educator starts his or her day with a belief that all students can learn. Sometimes events or circumstances undermine that belief, and the best way to alter that is through a collective, systematic approach to managing behavior and, by extension, learning. A systems thinking approach that all educators embrace is a necessary requirement to attain this goal. Consider how Fisher and Frey (2015) describe what systems thinkers do and how they behave: "The systems thinking classroom requires educators to consider the elements that impact student learning and design structures to leverage these elements" (p. 2). These structures owned by an entire school faculty allow for collaboration and collective efficacy. There are enough influencers of student learning (for example, home life, socioeconomic status, and personal motivation) beyond the control of educators that educators must work to enhance the impact of those elements they can control.

Throughout this book, I attempt to link the four principles of systems thinking with the work of managing learning in order to best prepare this book's readers for the thinking work they will need to do as they seek, gather, discuss, and respond to students' reactions to their instructional delivery. Table I.1 illustrates the four principles of systems thinking and their alignment to managing learning.

Table I.1: Aligning Principles of Systems Thinking to Managing Learning

Principle of Systems Thinking	Alignment to Managing Learning
Relationships	When students believe the adults within the learning organization are both invested in their learning and view negative behaviors as temporary obstacles, students will more readily invest in their learning. Every student needs an adult champion at school. I have yet to meet a student who has this connection (a strong, positive relationship with at least one educator) who does not make the progress teachers expect in school.
Communication	How teachers communicate among themselves, and with students, about students' behavior can affect student progress toward their behavioral and academic goals. As teachers discuss students and their behavior, they should do so with an eye toward improving outcomes and consolidating beliefs.
Responsiveness	Teachers act responsively by ensuring all students have access to the behavioral supports they need to allow them to work toward performing the desired behaviors with proficiency. Teachers should be aware of, and know how to respond appropriately to, the student behaviors that can occur as a result of a variety of antecedents. They also must not escalate the behaviors through their personal responses to them.
Sustainability	Ensuring teachers and administrators have a common set of expectations and respond to student behaviors with consistency will ensure sustainable behavior management. When all adult stakeholders understand that consequence in isolation is not instruction, they can work together to create a plan that pairs consequence and instruction to create sustainable learning that every student can readily understand at his or her current level of demonstration.

After reading the descriptions in table I.1 (page 5) of how the four principles of systems thinking align with managing learning, reflect on your own strengths as an individual and as part of a team. Consider where you have opportunities for growth. I encourage you to jot down some initial thoughts before you begin your journey through the chapters that follow.

About This Book

I have designed this book for all audiences regardless of grade level, curricular area, or role in education. Individuals and collaborative teams alike can benefit from exposure to the ideas in this book. The greatest benefit, however, will transpire when all members of a school community share a collective commitment to the work.

Chapter 1 lays the foundation for the managing learning element of systems thinking, highlighting the need for a collective approach to behavior management initiatives. Chapters 2–5 guide you through the process of building a positive learning environment as the best approach to managing learning and responding to negative behaviors. Chapter 2 focuses on building teacher-student relationships. Chapter 3 then examines ways to productively support group and peer interactions. Chapter 4 focuses on building positivity and offers suggestions for behavior management tools and strategies that will help teachers create a positive learning environment. Chapter 5 centers on how to specifically assess and address problem behaviors in the classroom, in the event that the concepts offered in the preceding chapters have not eliminated undesirable behaviors. Each chapter ends with a list of takeaways that summarize key points and prompts that ask you to reflect on your next steps as you plan the days and weeks ahead.

The appendix offers a unique glimpse into a school implementing a pilot program to address behavioral gaps. This case study provides an example of what is possible for all schools to achieve when they have a collective commitment to create a positive culture for addressing student behavior. I intend for the sample model to support school teams in their understanding, developing, and implementing the notion of managing learning.

The following chapters may produce a variety of personal reflections and reactions. You will no doubt find some affirmations of current practices you and your team have in place. Readers may also occasionally identify connections in the text to their personal experiences, resulting in the need to tweak a practice to further enhance what they do for students. Engaging with the text may also raise additional questions for teams to discuss. My hope is that this book will feed your desire to take the next step in improving student outcomes through classroom management practices.

Introduction

In chapter 6, "Managing Learning," of *Unstoppable Learning: Seven Essential Elements to Unleash Student Potential*, Fisher and Frey (2015) offer three questions that speak to how the structure of a system generates the behavior for that system. Before moving on to chapter 1, consider these questions:

- What is the relationship between the structures of my classroom and the learning and social behaviors I see?
- What are the short- and long-term consequences of the actions I take or do not take in regard to student behavior and the learning environment?
- Are there unintended consequences to the actions I take or do not take? (p. 150)

Have these three questions on a note card or in another readily handy place as you dive deeper into the content throughout this book, and think about how you will create the necessary elements that will minimize the impact of negative behaviors on your engaging instruction.

CHAPTER 1

IMPROVING BEHAVIOR MANAGEMENT THROUGH CULTURAL CHANGE

People don't buy what you do, they buy why you do it.

—Simon Sinek

Many of this book's readers will have had a similar experience to mine—you've been in school for the bulk of your life! If I count my years at university as time being in school, I have more than five decades of familiarity with a place called *school*. This means that many aspects of school feel comfortable, even those that are not effective. Dominique Smith, Douglas Fisher, and Nancy Frey (2015) explain how this familiarity affects our classroom management decisions:

> While our collective hearts as educators are in the right place, we tend to make decisions based on past experience. After all, we began our on-the-job training as teachers when we were five years old. Our beliefs about school, classroom management, and discipline have been shaped by decades of experience, starting in kindergarten (p. 2)

If you were to list ineffective practices that you have seen during your time connected to schools, what would you put on that list? Would your list include management strategies that involve overt disciplinary routines, humiliation, or sarcasm; structural components such as a specific number or length of courses, start and stop times, or the structure of the school calendar; or grading practices that include zeros, consequential grading, or penalty points? Here is what I am certain about—anything you could identify as ineffective practice in our profession could be filed under a one-word heading: *Easy*. Educators don't keep doing these things because they are effective; they do these things because they are easy, and oftentimes despite research that indicates otherwise and may even reveal the ineffectiveness of the practice. Consider education researcher and professor John Hattie's (2009) research on effect sizes, and in particular those practices that have a low, or negative, effect size, for example.

Among many ineffective practices identified, Hattie's (2009) research indicates that the practice of having students repeat a grade is one of a few common practices in education that has a negative impact, a loss of learning, on student outcomes. We don't use this practice because it works; we use it because it's an easier accounting practice. We really don't know what to do with a student who was not successful in all the components of grade 4. It's not wise to send him or her to grade 5, and we don't have a grade 4½ program (but we could if we wanted to and were prepared to move beyond what is easy). As another example, consider the school calendar that is still in vogue in most jurisdictions, which was designed for the agrarian cycle. We still subject students to an extended break despite the decreasing percentage of students involved in the agriculture industry ("Shortage of Farmers," 2014).

We have 21st century students being taught by 20th century adults using 19th century content on an 18th century calendar. This disconnect needs to be addressed well before we hit the midpoint of the 21st century. We need to push through the easy and get to the hard work in front of us. That's where our collective success truly lies. We can start by examining how we approach managing learning in our organization.

Contrary to what some may think of when they hear the phrase *managing learning*, the idea of managing learning does not imply imposing a restrictive environment, nor does it mean focusing on a power imbalance. Rather, it suggests creating the optimal learning environment that allows every student to experience success regardless of his or her current status, approach, baggage, or disposition. It implies that educators are responsible for organizing a physical space that helps cultivate a supportive and positive emotional space. However, because the traditional model of classroom management is predicated on control, we should not blame teachers when an environment is not conducive to all students' learning. Most veteran educators can recall a time when many believed that the most learning occurred in the quietest classrooms. Fisher and Frey (2015) recall this, suggesting, "Well-meaning teachers have been told to get their classrooms 'under control' by equally well-meaning principals" (p. 13) who believe that controlled classrooms where the adult is "in charge" will result in little misbehavior or disruptions due to students' fear of consequences or punishment. In reality, if a student wants to be a distruptor or class clown, he or she may challenge this control. This often leads to escalations educators have come to know as *power struggles*. Let's be clear; the educator holds the power in all these classroom situations. The only way the student can gain power is if the adult cedes it by engaging in the escalation (an escalation can't occur with only one participant).

So how do educators build positive learning environments? The answer is simple—with intentionality, or, in other words, on purpose. My experience in classrooms has proven that having an effective classroom policy (expectations, not rules) and the opportunity for students to learn from their actions (consequence plus instruction) ensure the positive learning environments teachers desire. This often requires a culture shift in a school. In this chapter, we will examine the relationship between culture and structures in a school, reflect on the importance of collective commitments to changing culture, and consider how teams should assess their current reality to make the necessary cultural changes.

Understanding Culture and Structure

Culture describes the assumptions, beliefs, values, and habits that guide the work of educators within a school. *Structure*, on the other hand, includes the policies, procedures, rules, and hierarchical relationships that exist within the school. Factors internal to the school may mostly drive culture, while factors external to the school influence structure. Great debate often ensues in schools and districts around which of these matters most for improving student learning outcomes. Some may argue that a strong, consistent structural approach will provide the stability that is a precursor to creating positive learning environments. Others may argue that the culture of the school, the way the adults treat each other and their students, and the consistency of instructional approach will lead to the desired learning environment.

What is clear is the notion that a school won't have success implementing structural change if the culture doesn't believe in change. Education researcher Phillip C. Schlechty (1997) states, "Structural change that is not supported by cultural change will eventually be overwhelmed by the culture, for it is in the culture that organizations find meaning and stability" (p. 136). If the existing culture does not have as an absolute that all students can learn at high levels, it is moot to have dialogue about some of the most effective teaching tools (formative assessment, response to intervention, and collaboration), as they won't produce the desired results in such a culture. Educational consultant Anthony Muhammad (2018) offers an even starker reality when he suggests:

> Terms like *research-based* and *best practice* have been no match for the deeply ingrained disbelief in student ability that cripples many struggling schools. In fact, I have had the opportunity to study several schools where pessimistic faculty members are eager to prove that new strategies or programs aimed at raising student performance do not work in order to justify and solidify their hypothesis that not all students are capable of achieving academic excellence. (p. 24)

If the prevailing culture devalues some students, clamping down on structure will do nothing to improve the outcomes for those students. This seems straightforward yet remains elusive in many jurisdictions. Muhammad (2018) provides some insight when he states:

> *Cultural change* is a much more difficult form of change to accomplish. . . . It takes knowledge of where a school has been, and agreement about where the school should go. It requires an ability to deal with beliefs, policies, and institutions that have been established to buffer educators from change and accountability. It is a tightrope act of major proportion. (p. 25)

This might lead one to think that the school or district leader should just decide how things ought to be done in a school and enforce this cultural change. However, Bryan Walker, partner and managing director of IDEO, and Sarah A. Soule (2017), professor of organizational behavior, suggest the exact opposite is really what needs to occur:

> Culture change can't be achieved through top-down mandate. It lives in the collective hearts and habits of people and their shared perception of "how things are done around here." Someone with authority can demand compliance, but they can't dictate optimism, trust, conviction, or creativity.

Collective commitment driven by meaningful dialogue is the precursor to any effective conversation about culture as well as structure. For example, a school may need to contemplate adding some additional behavior intervention time to produce the desired results, as behavior may be the single biggest deterrent to a student learning in the school. Educators gaining clarity on the culture (beliefs) will allow for the structure (schedule) change to succeed. Effective leaders understand this and build the collective commitment *with* their team, not *for* their team. Researcher Carol S. Dweck (2006) states these leaders "surround themselves with the most able people they can find, [and] they look squarely at their own mistakes and deficiencies" (p. 110). These types of leaders are not concerned with being the smartest person in the room or with achieving compliant behavior. They are concerned with growing their team's skills through a collective commitment, which impacts the growth of all students.

Ensuring that all staff members create and own the mission to serve all students is a critical component of the success in managing learning. Schools cannot address the needs of all students if there is misunderstanding, miscommunication, or misappropriation of the mission. It must be collectively established and reviewed annually in order to fully entrench the cultural changes required for successful, schoolwide ownership of managing learning.

Making a Collective Commitment to the Cultural Change

If we are going to change the culture, we have to understand this change doesn't take place overnight. Real change is a process, not a declaration—and it requires a collective commitment. Educational consultant Kenneth C. Williams and Tom Hierck (2015) suggest:

> Collective responsibility means much more than clichés, slogans, and catchphrases. It requires that the moral imperative (the why of your work) be embedded in every aspect of a school's culture—through every decision, behavior, and action taken as a school. (p. 9)

We can't think the culture has shifted just because we've created a fancy slogan that says we are about learning for *all* students, and posted it around the school. We need to focus on the space between posters and practice.

Change takes time. Sustainable change takes *more* time! I often suggest to schools that they should prepare for a three-year journey at a minimum. Year 1 is always about clarifying your purpose, your strengths, your journey, and your capacity. Schools must ask themselves if there is a collective commitment that all staff have created and own, or whether they have merely adopted a previous mission of the school that was handed down to them. It's important that staff actions and commitments are reflected in the mission they create. All educators need to be a part of this review of the mission and surface all their beliefs during this process. Modeling the expectations is a vital part of the work.

Year 2 is about aligning your behavior with the commitments you've made. Staff reflect on whether their policies, procedures, and practices align with the behaviors they are exhibiting. In content- or subject-area collaborative teams, teachers should review all that is occurring in their classrooms to see if it aligns with what is being espoused. Leaders should review with the entire faculty before considering or making changes.

Year 3 is about monitoring and celebrating. Educators need to reflect on what is working and what is not, and themselves—whether they can defend the work they are doing without becoming defensive. There also is a need for celebrations to occur as recognition of growth toward achieving the desired goal of managing learning. Every time there is a move forward, teams should intentionally acknowledge what has occurred. Here, they can begin to see the benefits of their efforts and know that what they are doing is working. For more information on the different roles, responsibilities, and stages involved in this process, with specific actions and steps different stakeholders can take to plan, manage, and nurture the collective work toward cultural change, see Williams and Hierck (2015).

It's important to acknowledge that lengthy and labor-intensive processes like implementing necessary cultural changes may not appeal to all school community members. Change can be daunting. The alternative—continuing to do the same things and get the same results—must be less desirable than the hard work ahead, or else schools won't move forward. Economist John Kenneth Galbraith (2001) frames this challenge best when he says, "Faced with the choice between changing one's mind and proving that there is no need to do so, almost everyone gets busy on the proof" (p. 241). Implicit in Galbraith's statement is the common argument I often hear from educators facing change initiatives: "We don't have the time." Few would disagree with this understandable argument; educators' time is stretched thin. Yet, if we are to achieve the necessary change, we must have the willingness to find a way. Unfortunately, the school community may always include those who will resist this work. Blank stares, foot dragging, and yeah-buts are the anchors that prevent any change in school. This is the behavior of the group Muhammad (2018) identifies as the Fundamentalists:

> Fundamentalists are the vanguards of tradition and protect the status quo. They are relentless in their attempts to discourage change and protect a system that has allowed them to function and thrive, and they organize to protect this traditional way of practice. . . . They view change itself as an enemy; therefore, anyone who challenges the system is a threat to the system and a threat to the Fundamentalists. They are the most aggressive and vocal combatants in this war of ideology. (p. 77)

Convincing Fundamentalists to change may seem insurmountable, but don't abandon hope. I do not believe anyone got into the education profession to be marginal or ineffective. If people have landed on those behaviors, it's often because someone condoned their behavior. Although the change process may be lengthy, time is on our side when we behave as a collaborative team that owns its collective commitment.

It's important to recognize how professional learning community (PLC) principles such as working in collaborative teams can support systems thinking elements and Unstoppable Learning principles. Collaboration enhances creation and analysis of these lists to ensure teachers share with each other what is working well with their students. As PLC architect Richard DuFour (2011) suggests:

> [Team members] share their expertise with one another and make that expertise available to all of the students served by the team. They establish clear benchmarks and agreed-on measures to monitor progress. They gather and jointly examine information regarding student learning to make more informed decisions and to enhance their practice. (p. 59)

Mutual trust borne out of a collective commitment results in open dialogues and a desire to add whatever practices it might take to mange learning. This needs to occur across all departments and grade levels, as DuFour (2011) reminds us when he describes how, in a PLC, "The school creates a *systematic* process that ensures that students who are struggling receive additional time and support for learning" (p. 61). When educators do this, all students will grow in their behavioral dispositions as well as their academic content.

Not only do educators work collaboratively in a PLC, but one of the big ideas driving the PLC process is that educators must "*take collective responsibility for the success of each student*" (DuFour, DuFour, Eaker, Many, & Mattos, 2016, p. 11). As educational consultant Jenni Donohoo (2017) states:

> When teachers believe that together they and their colleagues can impact student achievement, they share a sense of collective teacher efficacy. . . . Collective efficacy is high when teachers believe that the staff is capable of helping students master complex content, fostering students' creativity, and getting students to believe they can do well in school. (p. 3)

It's essential that every educator bear the commitment to any change initiative. We can no longer operate (and probably never should have operated) as individuals, each giving our best while trying to move all students forward.

The familiarity that educators have with established school routines, procedures, and practices can present a challenge to working collaboratively in teams and embracing change. If an individual feels he or she is well-versed in these aspects, and his or her results are "good," that person may find it difficult to accept that others have something else to offer. When I first started teaching, most teachers operated as independent contractors. They showed little desire to share best practice or to engage in cross-grade or cross-content conversations. I truly entered the profession being expected to figure things out for myself, and I suspect I am not alone in that experience. Unfortunately, this leads to a school of independent contractors whose only commonalities are the parking lot and the faculty lounge refrigerator. It creates districts of independent schools instead of coherent school districts, resulting in entirely different approaches to learning within the same jurisdiction.

It is simply impossible for any one staff member to be as smart, proficient, and effective as the collective staff. I can look back over my career and state unequivocally that anything *we* did was vastly superior to anything *I* did. Autonomy should reside in your method of delivery, not in what you deliver. Further, the strong desire to function as a team facilitates the move to talking about *our* students instead of *my* students. A strong, committed team will overcome challenges that a loose affiliation of individual talent will never surmount. Healthy and productive relationships among staff facilitate a positive school climate and learning environment and build healthy relationships among students and between students and staff. The strength of a team is that it becomes an unstoppable force, but an uncommitted individual can sink any team. All members of a team must buy into the analysis of the current reality and be part of the commitment to take the next step.

Assessing Your Current Reality

Clinical professor of educational leadership Marsha Speck (1996) has identified some key questions that I like to refer to as a test to see where schools would currently place themselves in terms of their collective commitments, especially those schools or individuals who have used the "lack of time" defense to stop progress. Following are some of the questions.

- What is the school vision?
- What are the skills or capacities needed to change?
- What are the incentives or motivations to change?
- What are the resources available to change?
- What is the action plan for change?
- What modifications need to be made during the change process or implementation of the action plan?
- How will the action plan for change be reviewed, evaluated, and revised?

These questions serve as a good assessment for educators to gauge their progress individually and collectively. If you ask the same questions and give the same answers as you did twenty years ago, it might be time to change how you assess your reality.

While beginning the change process will always require time, the adults in a school will realize that effort (and more) when they align their work in service of all students' learning. Schools exist as learning centers for children, not employment centers for adults. We cannot spend our time on proving why students can't learn or living on past glory. We must spend it on ensuring all students learn and we hold the keys to making that a reality.

Aligning the Classroom Culture

While every team member needs to be on board with the work ahead, it is equally important that every team member shares a common understanding of the team goals and aligns his or her practice to have consistency with all other team members. However, achieving consistency across your school or district seems to become a bigger challenge the larger a team is. It stands to reason that it is harder to get forty people to agree than it is to get four to. While this may be true, it should not deter schools or districts from pursuing this ultimate goal. What's at risk if you don't? Jennifer Medbery, founder and chief product officer for Kickboard, and Tom Hierck

(2017) suggest that in the absence of a schoolwide commitment with individual classrooms aligned to a broader purpose, silos of excellence will emerge:

> A consistent, student-centered, and restorative approach is essential for the effective implementation of a positive school culture initiative. Individual, classroom-based approaches are more likely to result in inconsistent expectations for students, a lack of teacher-to-teacher conversations about successful methods, and unnecessary escalation in student discipline, leading to silos of excellence rather than overall excellence. (p. 1)

Unfortunately, despite the potential for teams to become an unstoppable force, some individuals hang on to past comfortable practices and spend more time naming, blaming, and shaming than actually altering outcomes. These individuals often become what Muhammad (2018) describes as Survivors: educators who have "completely given up on practicing effective instruction" (p. 69). They can have a devastating impact on learning outcomes—and on their colleagues. Muhammad (2018) goes on to describe the depth of this impact, explaining, "Poor and ineffective instruction can completely undermine the school's fundamental mission" (p. 69). Michael Fullan (2007) and Nina Bascia and Andy Hargreaves (2000) validate Muhammad's (2018) notion of resistance to change and suggest that building a collective culture will support the positive intentions of schools and build some internal accountability for the desired results.

It does not matter how individually talented any person is if not all team members have a collective willingness to overcome the challenges their school faces. A strong, committed team will always perform better than a loose affiliation of talented individuals (Eaker & Keating, 2008). While recognizing the negative impact of resisters, Fullan (2007) says they also deserve respect both because they present ideas we might otherwise miss and because their influence is crucial to navigating the politics of implementation.

Tom Hierck and educational consultant Chris Weber (2014) offer the following list of essential beliefs or alignments needed from every teacher in creating a positive classroom culture:

- All students are valued and expected to make significant gains in their learning.
- Factors that may inhibit successful gains are temporary obstacles and challenges.
- All staff members accept responsibility for all students: students in other classrooms, students in other grade levels, students with disabilities, and students who speak another language at home.

- The status quo is never accepted; students' expectations are set appropriately and staff members recognize continuous improvement as the habit of great organizations.
- Change is an opportunity and all variables are considered.
- School leaders and educators view adult behaviors as having the most effective and significant influence on student learning and behaviors. (p. 114)

If these are not part of the collective commitment of the entire school team, the challenge of managing learning and improving behavioral outcomes for all students will be lost. It becomes easier, for example, to suggest that instead of the belief implied in the second bullet in the preceding list, educators ought to expect that external influences will have major impact and can be part of the excuse to explain a lack of student success. In order to ensure all educators are on the same page, collaborative teams should first reflect on these items together, and then entire faculties should collectively reflect as well. Building a positive classroom culture takes time and a commitment by all, to all.

The Takeaways

This chapter spoke to how a collective commitment to cultural change improves management of student behaviors. The power of the group in effecting change is critical. The key ideas from this chapter include the following.

- While culture is more important than structure, it can't be imposed and must be nurtured.
- Schools exist as learning centers for students, and educators need to take the time to make that a reality.
- To avoid creating pockets of excellence (success limited to some teachers or some classrooms but not all) and instead begin creating schools of excellence, all educators have to bear the collective commitment to cultural change.
- Ineffective practice often continues because it's easier than change.
- Healthy and productive relationships among staff facilitate a positive school climate and learning environment. *We* is greater than *me*!

Before moving on to the next chapter, please use the reproducible "Practices That Promote Positive Outcomes" (page 19) to create a list of all the current practices that exist in classrooms at your school that promote positive outcomes, and determine how many are systematic practices and how many are individual teacher practices. Discuss in your collaborative teams, and as a whole staff, which successful individual practices you might want to make systemic.

Practices That Promote Positive Outcomes

Create a list of all the current practices that exist in classrooms at your school that promote positive outcomes. Then, determine how many of these are systematic practices and how many are individual teacher practices.

Current classroom practices that promote positive outcomes:

-
-
-
-
-
-
-
-
-
-
-
-
-

Systematic Practices	Individual Teacher Practices
•	•
•	•
•	•
•	•
•	•
•	•
•	•
•	•
•	•
•	•
•	•
•	•
•	•

CHAPTER 2

SUPPORTING TEACHER-STUDENT RELATIONSHIPS

Develop strong relationships with students, and then lean on those relationships to establish expectations for students.

—Douglas Fisher and Nancy Frey

Nearly every teacher has likely encountered a former student who is now achieving unanticipated success and has been thanked by the former student for the role he or she played in the student's life. When teachers share these stories with me, I find it fascinating that the stories often reveal the significant moments between these students and teachers had very little to do with pedagogy or subject specificity. I can't imagine any of my former students remarking that when they learned how to balance chemical equations, the heavens opened up, and the light shone down on them, propelling them upward to unprecedented heights. Invariably, the significant moments occurred when teachers engaged or nurtured students or let students know the teachers were there if needed. These teachers reminded students what they could do, not what they couldn't. That's the essence of the work we do as difference makers.

Fisher and Frey (2015) suggest that students inevitably will grow if the adults connect with them, highlighting that there is "usually a relationship between whom you spend your time with and their academic progress" (p. 133). They also explain that there is a "difference between learners who feel valued and involved and those who are marginalized and therefore find ways to distance themselves from the environment" (Fisher & Frey, 2015, p. 131). Every student needs an adult champion in school, and every student will benefit from that connection. That is why strong teacher-student relationships are essential to fulfilling the larger systems thinking principle of relationships that supports Unstoppable Learning. The teacher should set the tone for the relationships among students and between the students and the teacher. To ensure this occurs in all classrooms and across all schools, we need to clearly express what we expect of students, and employ strategies that help us know our students well and convey to them that we are invested in their success. This chapter presents guidance for doing both.

Expectations, Not Rules

In *Seven Keys to a Positive Learning Environment in Your Classroom* (Hierck, 2017), I define the first key as *common expectations*. I go on to delineate that expectations serve as guidelines that are important not only in the classroom but, more often than not, also in life beyond the classroom's four walls. On the other hand, rules tend to be specific and are often responses to previous negative outcomes; they tend to be reactionary and often do not bring about the desired change. Building a positive learning culture is key to promoting student success academically and behaviorally. Developing positive teacher-student relationships is one of the most effective steps an educator can take toward achieving this positive learning culture. And establishing expectations allows the positive culture to emerge and thrive. This involves both setting expectations for students and managing the timing of these expectations.

Setting Expectations

When setting expectations for students, teachers should dispel the notion that when students come to the classroom, they know how to behave in accordance with the expectations of that teacher or that school. Many students simply do not know how to meet the expectations because those expectations have not been expressed to them explicitly. It's important to let students know the expectations in what I refer to as "our house." While students may have a home outside of school that has a certain set of expectations, we should establish the specific expectations for when they come to school—our house. These may look different from the expectations in their other house, but that should not preclude educators from establishing, and teaching, the expectations in school. As we work to teach and encourage the behaviors that are needed for success, we can (and should) identify and teach the expectations we want to see. Teachers cannot change the home each student goes to, and they have no control over students' world outside the school, but as teachers see students daily, weekly, and monthly during the school year, they can provide each student with skills to close the learning gaps.

When I work in a high school, I am often amazed to hear that the lunchroom is a source of problem behavior. Inevitably, schools assume that all students know how to eat meals and act responsibly after they have finished eating. They appear to make this assumption despite the evidence they have to the contrary—the repeated instances of problem behavior in the lunchroom. We know that many students might just as likely be eating in front of the television as at a table. Many students' experiences eating outside of the home are limited to fast-food restaurants. These are not locations that place high expectations on cleaning up after eating, returning trays and pushing in chairs, or speaking in conversational tones. Return to my "our house" analogy, and commit to teaching students what you expect in your school. Smith et al. (2015) suggest:

> It's far too common in schools for educators to wait for discipline problems to emerge and then handle them on a case-by-case basis. Such an approach leaves adults exhausted and children with limited skills development. We don't leave the acquisition of reading or mathematics skills to chance; we engage in explicit, systematic, and intentional instruction to ensure that learners progress academically. (p. 6)

Let's commit to teaching first and discussing consequences as a rare future occurrence.

The notion of our house has the potential to cause some friction in students' homes if parents or guardians believe it makes a value judgment about their homes. It's vital that schools communicate to students and their families that no one is suggesting that the expectations they have in their home environment are wrong. In fact, it is because we *don't* often have any control regarding what goes on in the home that we must spend time teaching the desired behaviors. Clearly, because we have roughly 25 to 40 (or more) students in our classrooms and 500 to 3,500 (or more) students in our schools, we need to have different expectations and need to see a different set of behaviors from what might be the norm at home.

Fisher and Frey (2015) have summarized these behavior management expectations in three simple statements:

1. Take care of yourself.
2. Take care of each other.
3. Take care of this place. (p. 135)

Fisher and Frey (2015) believe students can translate their situational concerns in their school through these statements, and they go on to suggest that educators should frame their school expectations around the following five key points (see Madden, 2014).

1. **Be clear about what you want:** Having clarity about what you expect is both desirable and helpful for your students and colleagues.
2. **Ask for clarifying questions up front:** Let others ask questions about specifications, resources, or timelines, and let them know you are open to these clarifying questions.
3. **Avoid managing the *how*:** Don't micromanage; let people get on with their work. Be open to their way of managing the work.

4. **Assist in removing obstructions and overcoming obstacles:** Assistance in the form of removing barriers is better than doing others' work for them.
5. **Manage the outcomes:** Manage the outcomes so the work is done in an effective manner. Creating milestones or using a checklist could facilitate this work.

This is not about suggesting parents lack skills but about setting a different set of expected behaviors in our house.

Managing Timing of Expectations

As each school year begins, it comes with a sense of newness, and this affords teachers an opportunity to build expectations into the classroom culture. Teachers need to take the time during this back-to-school period to establish and reinforce what they want or need to see in order for a positive learning environment to thrive. The best time to do this is the start of the school year. The next-best time? Right now!

The first days of class should provide clarity on the positive learning environment the teacher seeks in order to maximize all students' learning experiences. This is not to suggest that teachers should fill day one with a list of *thou shalt nots*. Teachers should think about how best to build the first day and what message each student should take home so he or she is eager to experience another day.

As the year unfolds, teachers should remain cognizant of breaks that occur, such as those around holidays or professional learning days, when educators are out learning more about their craft. These breaks in routine may result in students' losing their focus on the desired outcomes. Every school I've worked in has educators who can identify when an increase in office referrals occurs. This tends to happen around reporting periods, breaks (long and short), holidays, February in many American and Canadian schools (often related to postholiday energy slumps or, in some regions, the midwinter blahs), or even full moons. Here's the thing—we are aware of all these times, and they largely appear like clockwork on school calendars. Rather than simply acknowledging students and getting frustrated by a lack of student compliance, we may take these times to apply "booster shots" to remind students of the classroom expectations. Even the best-behaved students will need to review and practice the expectations and learn some new routines. When we do this as a whole-school endeavor, the likelihood of success is much higher.

Fisher and Frey (2015), citing the work of professor of education H. Jerome Freiberg (2013) suggest, "Students who feel confident in themselves and secure in their environments are able to learn more than those who do not" (p. 132). However, the amount of time educators have at their disposal to establish this positive environment is often a point of contention. Educators may look at the myriad of expectations that face them at the start of a typical school year and wonder whether taking some of that time to build relationships is worth the investment. While my anecdotal evidence from a variety of schools would suggest doing this has a huge upside, if there are teachers who still feel resistant to doing this work, at a minimum, I would ask that they track the amount of time they spend trying to retroactively build relationships or the time they lose as a result of damaged relationships with students. Based on my decades as an educator, I feel comfortable predicting that it will rapidly accumulate and often exceed the amount of time that they might have invested at the start of the school year.

Strategies for Improving Teacher-Student Relationships

As Fisher and Frey (2015) assert, "Want to raise levels of student achievement? Improve the quality of teacher-student" relationships (p. 149). Educators are always looking for new strategies to help with building positive and effective relationships with their students. The four strategies identified in the following sections are not meant to represent the complete list, but they are four that yield strong results and provide opportunities for teachers to build relationships while simultaneously establishing expectations with students.

Significant 72

Woodridge School District 68 is a district outside Chicago that has spent considerable time building relationships between students and teachers. The district calls its approach *Significant 72*, and it strictly devotes the first three days of school (seventy-two hours) to building effective relationships (Hierck, 2017). This practice relates directly to the effect size of 0.72 Hattie (2009) identifies in *Visible Learning* for teacher-student relationships.

The term *effect size* refers to a simple way of quantifying the difference between two data sets. Effect size emphasizes the size of the difference. Hattie (2009) introduced this notion as part of a mathematical formulation based on his analysis of a variety of influences educators engage in to impact student learning outcomes. He identified the hinge point of 0.40 as it relates to a typical year of instruction and went on to suggest that this equates to twelve months of growth for a student. In other words, students grow the equivalent of a year in learning outcomes when they spend a year in school. By extension, the effect size of 0.72 for teacher-student relationships is equivalent to almost twenty-two months of growth during that same school year.

These data clearly support the notion that it's essential teachers know their students individually, students know their teachers, and students know each other. Once teachers establish relationships with their students individually, as Significant 72 aims to do, and know how they can best teach and respond to each student, teaching and learning will substantially improve (Hierck, 2017). I am not saying the gains in attendance and achievement and the decreases in negative behaviors that the Woodridge staff have witnessed occurred simply because teachers built more effective relationships. However, I am willing to say that was the needed precursor for those changes. When teachers learn more about their students, they begin to see students individually and adjust their practice to meet the needs of each student, as they know more about those needs. A student who feels that the teacher seems genuinely concerned about him or her as an individual will change his or her response toward that teacher and demonstrate more effort and commitment than he or she might with another teacher in the same school (Varga, 2017). Haven't we all seen a teacher who manages to connect with a student whom many of his or her colleagues could not reach? The quality of the teacher-student relationship matters when it comes to effecting change.

One of the top effect sizes on Hattie's (2009) list of practices that affect student achievement corresponds to teacher credibility. The basic notion of teacher credibility is that students' *belief* that teachers know what they are talking about has almost eight times the impact that teachers' *actual knowledge* of what they are talking about does (Hattie, 2009). Relationships positively influence this belief—students get a greater sense of teacher credibility when teachers take time to get to know them personally. So what does it take to have teacher credibility? Hattie (2009) identifies the following four key factors.

1. **Trust:** Trust must be earned and can't just be expected. How teachers build trust is a function of many variables (teachers' own personal skills, those of their students, the culture of their schools) but it's important that students believe that teachers care about their personal as well as their academic development. And, as the old adage goes, trust is a two-way street; teachers need to trust students as well as build their trust. Earn trust by showing trust toward pupils.

2. **Competence:** If we expect our students to come to class prepared and ready to learn, it should be reasonable to expect the same of our educators. Teachers should reflect on the following questions: Are you organized for the day's lessons? Do your students believe you know your stuff? If you don't, is it okay in your classroom to say so and work with students to find solutions?

3. **Dynamism:** Teachers should consider whether their students see their passion for the work they do or the content they deliver. Enthusiasm is infectious! My best teacher recollections are of those educators who were enthralled by their content and got us students equally excited. Reflect on the following question: Do you build in your students a strong desire to learn despite current (temporary) struggles that result in them being as excited about the content as you appear to be?

4. **Immediacy:** Teachers can improve student relationships by increasing physical access in the classroom. Consider whether desk arrangement or other furniture creates physical obstacles in the classroom that impede students' ability to connect with the teacher. I can recall early in my own children's

school lives when they were surprised to see their teachers outside of school; almost as if they thought teachers were permanently planted behind a desk!

It's important to also recognize relationship building is not an either-or proposition. Educators should not choose between either building relationships with students or ensuring students have access to content. Instead, they should build them as part of the pathway to more effectively access the content. To achieve this goal and keep the momentum of Significant 72 going, Woodridge schools follow up these first three days with seventy-two minutes of assemblies every month geared toward the positive outcomes of relationship building. They encourage staff to find seventy-two seconds every day to acknowledge efforts to foster and further relationships. For more information on Significant 72, see Williams and Hierck (2015).

Investment Friend

Denise Johnson, an elementary teacher in Blount County, Alabama, shared with me a project she began called Investment Friend (personal communication, April 2013). This is somewhat of an adaptation of Significant 72. In this project, teachers identified those students who were struggling or going through a difficult time and took them on as their *investment friends* (IFs). Teachers built relationships with these students to ensure an investment in each student's future. The short acronym *IF* drove collegial conversations and individual teacher reflections through questions like, If I inserted myself in this student's life, what would change? and If I am looking for better outcomes from this student, what can I provide to him or her?

The most significant result of this project was a deeper connection between adults and students. In some instances, the connection continued after the student moved to the next school (as students would drop by a teacher's classroom to say hello, or would invite their IF to their graduation). While, as with any relationship-building activity, it can be difficult to prove that a specific action directly caused a specific outcome, significant improvements in areas such as attendance and achievement are harder to attain when students don't have connections to adults. As mentioned earlier, I have yet to meet a student who has a strong relationship with an educator in his or her school, who disappoints. And as Smith et al. (2015) indicate, "When students have strong, trusting relationships both with the adults in the school and with their peers, and when their lessons are interesting and relevant, it's harder for them to misbehave" (pp. 2–3). If you build relationships, every student at every grade level can learn.

Student Greetings

As I think about the learning spaces students enter, I am often drawn back to one of the most powerful quotes I heard early in my teaching career. Child psychologist and parent educator Haim G. Ginott (1972) says:

> I have come to a frightening conclusion. I am the decisive element in the classroom. It's my personal approach that creates the climate.

> It is my daily mood that makes the weather. As a teacher, I possess tremendous power to make a child's life miserable or joyous. I can humiliate or humor, hurt or heal. In all situations, it is my response that decides whether a crisis will be escalated or de-escalated, and a child humanized or de-humanized. (p. 13)

Teachers determine the weather in their classrooms, and this has significant impact on the climate. If you are aware of cold zones in your school, what have you done to change them?

One thing teachers can do that has a strong influence on the weather in classrooms is ensure students feel welcome. Fisher and Frey (2015) emphasize the importance of teachers' greeting their students before class and suggest a variety of what they call *four H greetings*, which teachers can choose from based on their personal communication-style preference: hello, high five, handshake, or asking how they are. They suggest to educators, "Think of these greetings and casual interactions as deposits you're making into [students'] emotional accounts. If and when problems arise in the future, you'll have something to draw on" (Fisher & Frey, 2015, p. 132). Teachers can pick the approach that they find most comfortable, but they do need to invest in some type of approach.

Welcoming is especially important for building relationships with students who join the class in the middle of the school year. Hattie (2009) identifies student mobility as having one of the most negative effect sizes impacting student learning outcomes, and he has determined this to have an effect size of –0.34. That minus sign in front of the number indicates that student mobility causes a loss of learning. It is understood that schools and educators have no control over if students switch schools a number of times during their academic careers, and it's easily understood why that has a negative impact on mathematics and reading. But a school does have control over how it welcomes these new students. Hattie (2009) suggests schools can mitigate the negative impact of mobility by working to ensure students feel welcome and supporting relationship building in the classroom.

A Show of Enthusiasm

Let's be clear; eyes are on you every day at school. Students are taking in information and receiving cues from how the adults comport themselves. Fisher and Frey (2015) suggest that educators should smile, display a sense of humor, and demonstrate enthusiasm for what they do, explaining, "As humans, we are hardwired to attend scrupulously to the facial expressions, gestures, and movement of others" (p. 134). However, it's equally important that you know yourself and express enthusiasm in a sincere way. If you are the kind of person who greets everyone with "Good morning!" and a big smile, keep doing it, as that reveals something genuine about your personality. If you're not that person, don't force it. Students will know if a smile is fake and the greeting insincere. Focus on what you can do to show your enthusiasm while remembering students are always observing you.

Another way educators can show enthusiasm is by having an interest in something that interests students. As a by-product of the Internet, and the ability to access information, it's now possible for students to know significantly more about a topic than any adult. Take Pokémon, for example. While some educators may have deeper knowledge of this than most, the average educator would likely know less than his or her students do. However, access to the Internet allows you to do research. Imagine the connection you could build with a student who is fascinated by Pokémon if you shared that Satoshi Tajiri invented the game Pokémon to replicate the bug-collecting games of his childhood (Eldred-Cohen, 2017). Showing enthusiasm for students' interests can also apply to activities students engage in outside your class. They always appreciate seeing their teachers at events that are important to them, including school plays, band concerts, and athletic games.

The Takeaways

Fisher and Frey (2015) believe "The classroom is a complex organizational structure that an adult who has a tremendous influence on the learning climate orchestrates" (p. 131). However, while the educator can exert influence, this myriad of interactions can't be controlled, nor can the role of the educator be to simply keep students safe and warm. Setting the tone, modeling the expectations, and celebrating the achievements are all essential in building effective relationships. The relationship between student and teacher drives all other relationships in the classroom and the school. The key ideas from this chapter include the following.

- A positive learning environment is the route to student success, and all educators should make immediately establishing that environment a priority.
- Engaging in relationship building reinforces Hattie's (2009) four components of teacher credibility (trust, competence, dynamism, and immediacy).
- Teachers are responsible for the climate of their classrooms and should think about their personal style and how it welcomes students.
- Educators should show their passion for this work and their inherent belief in being difference makers.
- Expectations guide actions for a lifetime, while rules guide behaviors in the short term.

Before moving on to the next chapter, please consider how you would reframe your current school rules as expectations. What impact might this change have?

CHAPTER 3

SUPPORTING GROUP INTERACTIONS AND PEER RELATIONSHIPS

Pedagogies and strategies matter, but students work hard for teachers they like. And they like teachers they know.

—Chris Weber

I believe relationships are the linchpin for everything else that happens in a school. They have just that much significance. Chris Weber (2018) cites a personal communication with educational consultant Jim Wright who suggests, "Students are more likely to act out in response to classroom influences: they try to escape or avoid difficult work, are bored with instruction, or desperately try to manage their image in peer interactions" (personal communication, May 23, 2017, as cited in Weber, 2018, p. 45). The notion that students' group status has a powerful influence on their behavior is a factor teachers must deal with. In the various roles I have held in education, it was an absolute truism that students will value their peers over the adults when the downward behavior spiral occurs. However, supporting student relationships will only work when the adults in the school are as invested in student relationships as the students themselves are. As Medbery and Hierck (2017) state, "An invested, purpose-driven staff is essential to attaining the consistent, student-centered, and restorative approach required to bring about a positive school culture" (p. 3). As students develop relationships with peers, they look to the adults to see how they model these relationships. Educational consultants Cassandra Erkens, Tom Schimmer, and Nicole Dimich Vagle (2018) clarify this by suggesting, "*Who* teachers are teaching matters more than *what* they are teaching, since teachers can't authentically get to *what* until they attend to *who*" (p. 13). It's important that we devote time, our most precious resource in education, to the power of relationships.

This attitude and approach influences students as they build connections. The National Scientific Council on the Developing Child (2105) suggests, "Extensive evidence collected over decades of research points toward the powerful influence of a composite of personal, relational, and contextual factors that are associated with positive outcomes in the face of adversity" (p. 10). For this reason, teachers must pay special attention to group dynamics and assignments in their classrooms. Educators often feel they face a binary choice between assigning group work and assigning individual work, and they may believe that one is exceedingly better than the other. In reality, both options have benefits, and we must keep that at the forefront when assigning work. This chapter will, however, focus on the dynamics of groups and how peer relationships have a significant impact on the culture and climate of every school and, by extension, the approach adults in the school take to managing behavior and cultivating the desired behavioral skills in all students. We will examine the benefits of group work and some cautions to be aware of when designing group work, consider strategies for peer relationship support, and reflect on the concept of behavior management as it applies specifically to groups.

Benefits of Group Work

Recall the three reflective questions (Fisher & Frey, 2015) for managing behavior and building relationships that I suggested readers refer to throughout their interaction with this text:

- What is the relationship between the structures of my classroom and the learning and social behaviors I see?
- What are the short- and long-term consequences of the actions I take or do not take in regard to student behavior and the learning environment?
- Are there unintended consequences to the actions I take or do not take? (p. 150)

This is a good place to revisit those questions as we look at group work. Working in groups can help students develop skills that may well be important for them in their lives beyond graduation. Positive group experiences have a positive impact on student learning, retention, and overall college success (National Survey of Student Engagement, 2016). When group activities are well designed and thought out, they can help students develop and reinforce skills that are relevant to not only group work but also individual work, including the ability to:

- Organize so that time is effectively managed
- Clarify and build personal understanding through discussion
- Give and receive effective feedback
- Develop communication skills

- Simplify tasks into manageable steps
- Challenge themselves to go deeper in their learning
- Develop a growth mindset
- Identify desirable learning attributes in others that they may also want to develop or, at least, learn from
- Work on conflict resolution skills while also learning to share their voice

When teachers take the time to develop group dynamics (the changing of behavior through interactions in the group) and teach the effective skills and steps of collaborative group work, it will lead to boundless learning outcomes. Instructional coach Alexis Wiggins (2017) describes the impact this work had as her students became more adept at working together:

> Through the feedback process, they began to flex and build the muscle of successful group work so that they were taking turns, apologizing for cutting each other off, practicing asking questions more regularly, and valuing the whole group's input. (pp. 131–132)

Wiggins (2017) also suggests these benefits of the group feedback process help eliminate a common challenge in group work: an imbalance in group members' contributions. Unequal student contributions in group assignments often cause academically strong students to view group work negatively. For many of our academically strongest students, group work seems like a punishment, as inevitably, they will participate to a higher degree than others, and they will work with someone they perceive as a threat to achieving the highest grade possible. When group dynamics are not well developed, group work can likewise lead to weaker students participating to lesser degrees than others.

According to the National Survey of Student Engagement (2006), ensuring that all students are engaged in their learning and in developing these skills has other benefits as well. The survey authors suggest what I believe are two key and desirable long-term benefits:

- Student engagement is positively related to first-year and senior student grades and to persistence between the first and second year of college.
- Student engagement has compensatory effects on grades and persistence of students from historically underserved backgrounds. (National Survey of Student Engagement, 2006, p. 13)

This aligns well with what Wiggins (2017) identifies as subsequent benefits of effective collaboration. She suggests "increased and better participation and enhanced communication and social skills" (Wiggins, 2017, p. 132) are the next two benefits that educators should expect to see blossom in their students.

Developing positive group dynamics and relying on the strength of the group to positively influence outcomes should be commonplace in all classrooms across all schools. English instructor Pham Huynh Phu Quy (2017) highlights this by suggesting that this effort "not only promotes a sense of confidence in students but also builds trust and acceptance among group members" (p. 20). Positive group dynamics won't occur by chance and will grow over time as students gain comfort and confidence in each other and in their environment.

Cautions About Group Work

Although group work has significant potential learning benefits, simply assigning group work comes with no guarantee that groups will achieve the learning goal. In fact, "group projects can—and often do—backfire badly when they are not designed, supervised, and assessed in a way that promotes meaningful teamwork and deep collaboration" (Carnegie Mellon University, n.d.). Cautions about three conditions of group work are in order at this point.

1. **Student selection:** Although it may seem advantageous to have students select whom they want to work with, this can cause students to become isolated (think of the student always picked last or assigned to a group by the teacher), students to develop groupthink (the "practice of thinking or making decisions as a group in a way that discourages creativity or individual responsibility," Oxford University Press, 2008, p. 550), or students to settle into roles (for example, one student is always the recorder, one is always the reporter, one is always the researcher, and so on).

2. **Set groups:** You should not have set groups for the entire school year. Just as student selection makes it easy for students to settle into roles and familiarity that may stymie growth opportunities as you stretch students, placing students in set groups also contributes to this phenomenon.

3. **The option to opt out:** You may have a student who wants to opt out of group work, as he or she feels more comfortable working alone. While I do not advocate teachers' being so rigid as to insist on this group structure, if students are to grow positively as collaborators and develop the collaboration skills that they will find essential going forward in their adult lives, they will need to work with others. You might initially make hesitant students' group smaller, but you should not allow students to opt out. Erkens et al. (2018) suggest teachers need to create "constructs for collaborative group work in which teams work together to reach a common goal, capitalize on each team member's strength, and achieve a greater purpose" (p. 31). Students cannot achieve this by working independently.

These conditions work to undermine the powerful impact of group work and can actually prevent the development of previously outlined critical skills that group work can foster under the correct conditions. In order to ensure group work does not stand in the way of this critical development, teachers should cultivate positive group dynamics by understanding and supporting peer relationships in the classroom.

Behavior and Groups

The next chapter will focus on behaviors and the challenges associated with maintaining a positive classroom culture while addressing behavioral concerns. In this section, I want to touch on group dynamics and the group approach—including both student groups and faculty groups—as avenues to explore for mitigating the impact of disruptive behavior. Educators must teach the behavioral expectations for student groups and group members as they teach the academic expectations. As educational consultants Austin Buffum, Mike Mattos, and Chris Weber (2009) point out, "Behavior and academic achievement are inextricably linked. A student's academic success in school is directly related to the student's attention, engagement, and behavior" (p. 111). We must teach what we expect across both the academic and behavioral realms. Doing so in group settings helps accomplish this by ensuring all students receive the same common message and expectations. School and district teams need to create the plans that will allow them to maximize the strength of student groups to ensure students achieve the desired outcomes. This begins with establishing clarity of purpose.

Unfortunately, as Smith et al. (2015) point out, "Traditional school discipline practices are considered separate from the academic mission of the school" (p. 5). Without a clear school purpose or, worse yet, with a purpose that is designed only for the easy-to-reach, easy-to-teach students, schools will suffer from what the business community calls *mission drift*—a move away from the organization's mission. Every school I have ever worked in throughout my thirty-five years in this profession has a mission statement, and educators often declare it proudly. Drift doesn't occur because of a lack of intent; it occurs because of a lack of adherence largely borne out of a lack of ownership of and dialogue about what matters most. Williams and Hierck (2015) further explain:

> Drift happens when schools don't live their mission—often when educators unconsciously separate the mission from the work. It's not about a lack of commitment or investment; it is about a lack of commitment to or investment in the right things. . . . What matters most is creating a school with an unrelenting focus on learning for all. (p. 6)

If your mission statement does not include the idea of challenging students to adhere to all your school's behavioral expectations, it might be time to re-examine the statement. If your mission statement says that you and your colleagues believe that all students can learn, does this reflect both social and academic behaviors? If you are able to respond affirmatively, ask yourself this question: Have you built time and opportunity into your schedule to gather as colleagues and talk about your collective response, aligned to your mission, when students are not yet proficient? Director of leadership development Sarah E. Fiarman (2016) talks about the power of this action when she says, "Making decisions collaboratively—about discipline, school policies, and family outreach strategies—provides the opportunity for others to point out our blind spots. When we work in isolation, it's hard to see what we don't see" (p. 14). However, collaborating in this way takes a high degree of collegiality and the willingness to be vulnerable. It takes a strong desire to maintain that unrelenting focus on learning and not reduce the discussion to the well-worn, well-rehearsed narrative of excuse making. Many of the readers of this book will be familiar with the concept of group norms as a method of ensuring the group stays focused and on task. The group should develop these norms collectively, and all members must agree to champion and adhere to these norms. In other words, it is not the task of the principal to ensure groups follow their agreed-on norms. Modeling the desired behaviors for students serves a strong function while also furthering the fluency of the adults in this practice, making it more comfortable for them to clarify the work for students.

Strategies for Peer Relationship Support

It's important that teachers focus on the relationships that exist within the classroom and devote instructional time to nurturing them. To reach the ultimate goal of producing students who can engage in meaningful dialogue while contributing to their communities as adults, teachers need to cultivate students' capacity to collaborate and teach students the benefits of working with others. While teachers spend a lot of time and energy on the very worthy and important pursuit of cultivating strong, effective teacher-student relationships, as noted in chapter 2 (page 21), I would argue based on my professional experience in schools that peer relationships are, at a minimum, as important as, and often more important than, teacher-student relationships. Think about a group of any thirty people randomly assigned to spend a significant portion of their day together. Is it reasonable to expect that they would all get along, share similar interests, and not need any support to develop individual and group cohesion? That rhetorical question does not need a response, as teachers know the significance of assisting in the development of peer-to-peer connections. This goes beyond serving as a referee to mediate disputes; it extends to modeling healthy relationships and helping students grow while developing healthy relationships. The following sections will explore specific strategies teachers can use to ensure they provide classroom experiences that support peer relationships.

Sociogram of Existing Relationships

To begin, teachers need to understand the existing peer relationship dynamics in their classrooms. Fisher and Frey (2015) suggest an activity that teachers can use to represent the three pre-existing affiliations in classrooms. Teachers begin by asking students the following questions, either privately or through individual written response:

1. **In-school social affiliations:** "Who are the people you usually eat lunch and play at recess with?"

2. **In-classroom work affiliations:** "Who are the three people in this class that you like to work with when you have a group assignment?"

3. **Out-of-school social affiliations:** "If you had a chance to take three people in this class to a movie (or to play with at your house), who would you invite?" (Fisher & Frey, 2015, p. 136)

After students respond anonymously or privately to these questions, teachers prepare a sociogram. A *sociogram* is a visual representation of the relationships within a group. It can illustrate, as in the example in figure 3.1, friendship patterns. Figure 3.1 represents these patterns, using circles for male students, rectangles for female students. Unidirectional arrows indicate one student responding positively to another student, and dual direction arrows indicate a positive response between both students. The connection of any one child to another or to the group as a whole is an example of information users can derive from a sociogram.

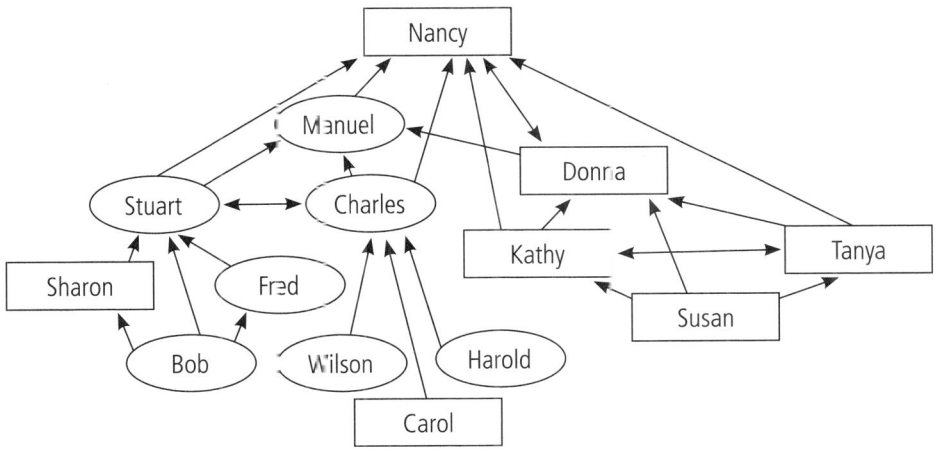

Figure 3.1: Sociogram example.

Teachers then tally how often each student is mentioned, placing those mentioned most often in the center of a series of concentric circles, and those least mentioned on the outermost circle. This provides an immediate visual of the social dynamics existing in the classroom. At this point, teachers might feel tempted to place the most isolated student with the most popular student, but experts contend this practice may actually exacerbate the issue and recommend educators avoid doing so (Murphy & Faulkner, 2000). Fisher and Frey (2015) propose, instead, that teachers number the students—for example, if a class featured thirty students, you would number them from 1 to 30—and then divide that list in half (1 to 15 and 16 to 30) before taking two students from each half (students 1 and 2 and students 16 and 17) to form a group of four. This will balance out the skill levels. Once groups form, teachers should monitor the group dynamics to ensure the focus remains on the task at hand and that social skill deficits don't derail achievement.

I like to conclude group work with having students reflect on these two questions.

1. What is one thing others in the group learned from you?
2. What is one thing we can do to make the group process better?

Teachers can use this information to structure future groups, respond to any concerns identified, and decide if any further instruction on group function or dynamics needs to occur.

Significant 72 Revisited

In chapter 2 (page 25), I wrote about the powerful impact the Significant 72 initiative has had in building teacher-student relationships in Woodridge School District 68. Attendance, academic achievement, and behavior data the district collected suggest positive impact in areas associated with effective peer relationships (Hierck, 2017); the evidence has shown desired outcomes such as increased empathy, decreased peer-to-peer aggression, decreased bullying, and increased social management. By continuing to refer back to relationships students built in the first few days of school and revisit content from beginning-of-the-year assemblies, educators can build and capitalize on the skills students have developed. If students are currently in conflict, asking them to go back to a time when they productively solved a problem can give them insights that may help with the current challenge.

Team Building and Class Building

With computers, Internet access, and continual advances in technology, teachers can no longer acceptably suggest that a lack of tools prevents them from implementing activities to build teams and the class as a whole. A variety of time- and cost-effective products and resources—including teacher strategies like Significant 72, which can be shared online, websites like Kagan Learning (www.kaganonline.com), and strategies and activities teachers share on Pinterest (www.pinterest.com)—exist to help teachers develop essential skills students need to help them see how their actions impact the classroom, learning, and relationships with others. These tools also provide opportunities for the adults to learn alongside their students in developing collaborative behavioral solutions and responsibility. However, while we should focus on improving the life chances of every child and not be satisfied with temporary compliance while he or she is in school, it's equally important that we, the adults, do not do all the work. Facilitating the growth of our students means just that—facilitating. As Erkens and colleagues (2018) state, "Schools should not be places where students go to watch teachers work exceptionally hard. The tables need to turn so students are doing more of the mental heavy lifting" (p. 35).

Educators should expect that students interact with each other in groups to meet their variety of social and emotional needs, get information, provide feedback, and generally hang out together. This behavior is not static, as each interaction in their group has the potential to influence the behavior of others, resulting in the possibility of continuous change. This is the essence of group dynamics. Teachers can use the notion that groups demand reciprocity among their members in a positive and proactive way to reinforce the idea of students taking responsibility for cultivating relationships and contributing equally to group work. Every group influences its members' behavior to a great extent.

Professor of sociology Janet Mancini Billson (1986) posits the idea that classrooms and small groups are one and the same and notes, "Deeper awareness of small group processes can enhance teaching effectiveness" (p. 143) and believes that "Every participant in a group is responsible for the outcome of the group interaction" (p. 144). Although the classroom leader has the ultimate responsibility, Billson (1986) suggests that students share a significant responsibility for this outcome as well, and recommends discussing that responsibility with students and exploring the possibility of letting students plan certain segments of the course together. This aligns well with what Hattie (2009) identifies as having one of the top effect sizes on student learning: self-reported grades and student expectations, which have an impact of 1.44, far above a typical year of instruction, which comes in at 0.40.

As I've noted previously, where educators and schools choose to invest their time indicates what they consider important. Think about whether you have time built into your daily or weekly school calendar for examining how frequently students access learning experiences that support this type of relationship building. If you find no such time in the current school schedule, make a change to include some opportunity, even if the change is small at first. For example, instead of tackling a schoolwide initiative, you can start with scheduling activities in your own classroom. Do you have an appropriate time during your lesson when students could use a brain break or the class could benefit from an activity designed to build connections? These brain breaks may be needed when it appears that attention is waning or off-task behavior (fidgeting, distracting others) is on the rise. Rather than a teacher or peers reacting to these events in a negative fashion (damaging rather than building relationships), the brain break provides a positive stimulus that may serve to strengthen the ties in a positive classroom culture. As a teacher, one of my favorite strategies to use for a brain break was the 5-4-3-2-1 strategy. In essence, the teacher thinks of various activities and has the students do those in descending order. For example, the teacher would say, "Do five jumping jacks, four handshakes, three hops, two walks around the classroom, and one high five with a peer." I would ensure pauses between each activity to ensure all were participating, and this often was enough to re-energize the students and regain focus in the classroom.

The more team and class building occurs, the more benefits begin to materialize, and the work grows from classroom to classroom as educators take an interest in the success they see in colleagues' classrooms.

Cooperative Learning

Cooperative learning is an approach whereby teachers organize their classroom activities into academic and social learning experiences. This approach moves beyond merely arranging students into groups. It aims to structure positive interdependence by having students collectively work in groups to complete tasks toward the learning goals. Cooperative learning tasks should be rigorous and open-ended and allow for student creativity. When learning remains individual, the classroom can become a hotbed of competition. When learning becomes cooperative, students can capitalize on each other's skills and strengths (for example, students can take on different roles, like content resource, peer assessor, or progress monitor, using a rubric). In this approach, the teacher also changes roles from dispenser of knowledge to facilitator of learning.

Clinical psychologist and education researcher Spencer Kagan (n.d.) has designed numerous teacher tools that assist teachers in developing a positive cooperative learning environment. He identifies four basic principles of cooperative learning and how they help optimize active engagement among students. These principles create the acronym *PIES* (Kagan, n.d.).

1. **Positive interdependence:** Positive interdependence has two components—(a) a positive correlation among outcomes and (b) a structure that requires contributions from all students. In other words, the collaborative learning should ensure that one student's gains will also help other students (for example, through peer encouragement of achievement and peer tutoring) and that all students' contributions are necessary for task completion.

2. **Individual accountability:** In a typical classroom lesson, teachers often include a block of time to pose general questions to the entire class. This generates the usual hands-in-the-air response, often from the same students. These students may be seeking teacher or peer approval, and this may seem to be an accurate format for individual accountability. The problem in this scenario is that it is restricted to an individual who volunteers to provide a response as opposed to all members of the class demonstrating individual accountability. The weak students, the confused students, the bored students are not called on and may be pleased about that. In order to truly achieve individual accountability, the teacher could instead engage in authentic formative and summative assessment individualized to each student as the learning progresses.

3. **Equal participation:** The third PIES principle, equal participation, results in more active engagement. Examine this scenario: a teacher has presented the pros and cons of an enduring social issue—capital punishment. When the activity begins and students share their perspectives in their teams, a predictable scenario unfolds. Students who are more articulate, outgoing, or enthralled by the subject tend to dominate the dialogue. Those at the opposite end of these traits contribute little to the dialogue. However, there are strategies to ensure equal participation. I used to ask each student two questions after any group effort: What did everyone in the group learn from you? and What can we do to make the group process better next time?

   Another example that I have seen modified from what Kagan (1994) called *concentric circles* is the inside-outside circle. In this activity, students form pairs and line up opposite each other, forming an inner and an outer circle. Either the inside or the outside circle students ask a question from their question card, and the student opposite to them answers. Students who delivered the question offer feedback. Then, partners switch roles and trade question cards. Inside circle students rotate clockwise to a new partner. Teachers can vary this rotation; students could rotate a single place over, or two places, or three.

4. **Simultaneous interaction:** The last PIES principle focuses not on students' equal amounts of active engagement but on the absolute amount of engagement—the percentage of students who are simultaneously engaged. Kagan (n.d.) notes, "Engagement can take the form of interaction (as when all students are in pairs interacting) or it can take the form of individual action (as when all students are writing at once)."

Kagan (n.d.) further explains, "When PIES are not in place, we are merely doing group work, not cooperative learning. Group work does not consistently produce active engagement by all, so the gains of cooperative learning are not assured." To help teachers evaluate whether they have these principles in play in their classrooms, Kagan (n.d.) has also identified critical questions that align with each principle, as shown in figure 3.2. Teachers should initially reflect on these questions independently, and then in teams. A positive answer to any of these questions indicates the corresponding principle is in place.

Principle	Critical Questions
Positive Interdependence	Does the success of one benefit others? Is everyone's contribution necessary?
Individual Accountability	Is individual, public performance required?
Equal Participation	How equal is the participation?
Simultaneous Interaction	What percent are interacting at once?

Source: Kagan, n.d.

Figure 3.2: Kagan's four principles and aligned critical questions.

When students experience these four principles, they feel like they are all on the same side of the learning equation, they can't hide during the lesson, they have equal status, and they are all engaged in the lesson, which are all important to cooperative learning.

The Takeaways

Educators cannot ignore the importance of group dynamics in promoting positive environments as they build their approach to managing learning. The key ideas from this chapter include the following.

- Both addressing individual needs and realizing the benefits of collaboration have a place in every classroom.
- All classrooms across all schools should have the goal of developing positive group dynamics and relying on the strength of the group to positively influence outcomes.
- Peer relationships are as important as, and often more important than, teacher-student relationships.
- Educators should expect that students interact with each other in groups to meet their variety of social and emotional needs, get information, and provide feedback. And educators should proactively build time into their daily or weekly school calendar for this interaction.

- Focusing on the four principles of (1) positive interdependence, (2) individual accountability, (3) equal participation, and (4) simultaneous interaction can help teachers build cooperative learning in classrooms (Kagan, n.d.).
- Making decisions as part of a collective counters the challenge of working alone: "It's hard to see what we don't see" (Fiarman, 2016, p. 14).

Before moving on to the next chapter, please reflect on what barriers prevent you and your team from functioning as a collective rather than a loose affiliation of individual talent.

CHAPTER 4

SUPPORTING A POSITIVE LEARNING ENVIRONMENT

We demonstrate personal support for others when we are responsive to needs, create a positive climate, and display interest in what others have to say.

—Douglas Fisher and Nancy Frey

According to the National School Climate Center (2010), a *positive climate* is one in which people feel socially, emotionally, and physically safe; are engaged and respected; and all work together toward common and meaningful goals. Creating this environment demands an all-hands-on-deck approach across all classrooms and all schools. Every student is a success story waiting to be told. The work of educators is to help students share, discover, or unleash their stories.

School climate affects a number of areas in schools. According to research analyst Darren Kwong and assistant professor of educational administration and secondary education Jonathan Ryan Davis (2015), chief among these are "teacher commitment, motivation to learn, student identity development, student dropout rates, sense of school community, school satisfaction, school violence, academic achievement, and higher scores on standardized tests" (pp. 68–69). In order to ensure they support these areas well, it follows that teachers should make creating a positive learning environment for all students a priority. In this chapter, we will examine the impact of teachers' intentionally choosing positivity in their daily work and attitudes, reflect on the link between positive learning environments and positive behavioral outcomes, explore the research-based best practice around positivity, and gain tools and strategies for fostering positive behaviors.

Positivity by Design

In the introduction to *Seven Keys to a Positive Learning Environment in Your Classroom*, Hierck (2017) identifies the importance of having a positive attitude as a critical first step in creating the optimal learning environment. He points out this challenge: "Creating a positive classroom learning environment is messy, uneven, complex, and necessary for all teachers to engage in" (Hierck, 2017, p. 5). As you read those words, think about your current, previous, or upcoming class. What elements of the class would lead you to believe that it might be messy, uneven, or complex? I believe it begins with the students in every classroom. Teachers need to accept that students are on a continuum of learning. Different content areas, topics, and learning activities will yield different strengths and challenges for each student. Their varying rates of growth, external supports or pressures, and readiness will add other degrees of separation and uniqueness to them as individuals. Hierck (2017) goes on to suggest two extremes in creating this optimal environment:

> At its most rewarding, it provides opportunities for teachers to have rich dialogue with their students as they collectively work to create environments that produce high levels of success for *all* students. At its most challenging, it creates frustration for teachers as they deal with factors related to demographics, home characteristics, and the existing school culture. At both extremes, maintaining a focus on the learning environment is critical. (pp. 5–6)

One of the true anachronisms in our profession is that the only factor we generally use when organizing students in schools is their age. This assumes that all twelve-year-olds are ready for grade 7 and have the same abilities in mathematics, English language arts, science, physical education, music, art, social responsibility, and behavior. In other words, this assumes students have no variation, and we can teach all students the same way, and they will respond positively to that one way. This would be akin to you and your colleagues heading out to lunch and having the restaurant's host stop you at the entrance to check your age. Having ascertained that, the host would assign seating based on age and ensure you did not sit with older adults (whose conversation would clearly be above you) or younger adults (whom you might corrupt or confuse). In reality, every classroom will contain so many unique student qualities and characteristics that it can't help but be messy, uneven, and complex. Even if all the students you had in class last year returned to your classroom again in the fall, the same messiness, unevenness, and complexity would result, as they (and you) would have changed over the summer break. The best approach for teachers to use when facing this messiness is to choose to be intentionally positive.

Being intentionally positive is not as easy as it might seem. It requires teachers to let go of one of our inherent human behaviors—the ability to see what does not fit. Let's say, for example, that one of the foundational expectations for your classroom is responsibility. When students enter your classroom and get settled in for the powerful learning that will unfold, you should acknowledge all the responsible behavior you see. But isn't it distracting, and all too tempting, to focus your attention on the student who is sitting slumped at his desk, book closed, with no supplies out? Let's be clear; every student wants to receive adults' time and recognition. If the slumped student only receives it through displaying negative behaviors, it should not surprise you that the negative behavior grows. The next day in class may well bring another student not ready to learn if he or she believes these types of behaviors will help him or her gain a teacher's time. It is critical that educators recognize and promote the behaviors they want to see most often. In this sample scenario, I am not suggesting that a teacher should ignore the student's lack of responsibility. I am suggesting he or she launch a brilliant lesson and get the student engaged. Then approach the student who is not on task, and ask him or her about the expectation of responsibility. As I will discuss further in chapter 5 (page 65), if the behavior appears to occur due to a lack of the requisite skill, do what you would do if this were an academic deficit—teach! It's essential that educators use what they indicate is important (in this example, responsibility) in a positive way to get the desired result, for example, by noticing when students are being responsible, and committing to teaching that behavior when students do not display it, as opposed to rushing to consequences. I choose to believe *all* students can learn the skills we endeavor to teach, and I work with positive intention to make that happen. Over my career, I have come to realize that while being positive does not guarantee a result, being negative sure does.

Positivity Outcomes

As Hierck and Kent Peterson (2017) note, "Positive climates arise from the practices and rituals implemented and encouraged within a school. Students learn appropriate behavior in the same way they learn how to read—through instruction, practice, feedback, and encouragement" (p. 6). They go on to suggest that the use of positive behavior management practices is related to the following outcomes:

- Student academic engagement
- Decreased disruptive behavior
- Increase in the intrinsic motivation of students
- Increased math and reading achievement
- Development of self-management skills
- Increased positive verbal interactions
- Decreased negative verbal interactions
- Decreased transition time
- Increased peer social acceptance
- Decreased referral rates
- Happier, more resilient students (Hierck & Peterson, 2017, p. 6)

Identifying the outcomes that are beneficial to student success is an important part of establishing the practices that they require. Teachers often face the dilemma of clarifying what behaviors lead to these outcomes.

In order to assist with this, Hierck and Peterson (2017) collected data sets over a seven-year period that chronicled more than 152 million behavior instances, as identified by teachers, at 645 schools. Following are the identified behaviors from those data that had a positive impact on students and their learning.

- Display of pride in one's school
- Collaboration
- Kindness
- Pride in one's work
- Leadership
- Helpfulness toward others
- Wise use of time
- Preparedness
- Love of learning
- Good decision making
- Active listening or engagement
- Cooperation
- Appropriate use of communication
- Care
- Self-reliance
- Perseverance or resilience
- Insightfulness
- Organization
- Action that goes above and beyond

When teachers intentionally notice and chronicle these behaviors, they instill a sense of positivity across the classroom and set the tone for effective behavioral instruction.

Research-Based Best Practice

What does the evidence suggest works best to manage classroom expectations and behavior? Let's not confuse best practice with the practice you are best at. Let's turn to the words of teacher and school leader Gianna Cassetta and researcher Brook Sawyer (2013):

> If we want students to be engaged learners, they need to be self-directed ones. We know that choice, inquiry, and collaboration are critical elements of instruction, but in order for students to participate positively, we must create predictable, relationship-driven classrooms where students learn to assume responsibility for their behavior and interactions. (p. 7)

As noted throughout the previous chapters, it's very important that students understand the expectations for behavior in the classroom. Each classroom is unique based on a variety of factors, such as grade level, content, demographics of the students, the adults providing the instruction and support, and parental support. Teachers should communicate the expectations for all the learning activities and predispositions they would like to see in their students. Identifying these for group learning, peer interactions, and individual work helps clarify for students what is needed to have a positive learning environment. Fisher and Frey (2015) identify expectations that exist at their school to address schoolwide citizenship, centered on four major themes:

1. **Welcoming:** Are you contributing to an inviting learning environment?
2. **Do no harm:** Are you contributing to a safe learning environment?
3. **Choice words:** Is your language positive and encouraging growth, remaining consistent with being welcoming and eliminating harm?
4. **Never too late to learn:** Are you an active participant in your own learning, and do you facilitate the learning of others?
(Fisher & Frey, 2015, p. 157)

Explaining these expectations to students is part of teachers' effective instructional delivery. Having students internalize them through clarity and reinforcement ensures these expectations become part of the fabric of school. Education systems should aim to ensure that every student learns and grows under their care, that every student has value added after each year in school, and that all students are prepared for their lives after school—whatever challenges may come their way. Classicist and university administrator Richard W. Livingstone (1941) suggested this decades ago when he asserted:

> The test of a successful education is not the amount of knowledge that a pupil takes away from school, but his appetite to know and his capacity to learn. If the school sends out children with a desire for knowledge and some idea of how to acquire and use it, it will have done its work. Too many leave school with the appetite killed and the mind loaded with undigested lumps of information. (p. 28)

Let's agree to have schools designed for children's futures and not their parents' pasts.

The Learning Pit

James Nottingham (n.d.), cofounder and director of Challenging Learning, created the Learning Challenge as a way to promote and enhance challenge and inquiry. This process supports students' productive struggle and can be applied to academic and behavioral struggle like. He articulated a four-step inquiry process (concept, conflict, construct, and consider) and aligned this with professors of education John B. Biggs and Kevin F. Collis's (1982) Structure of the Observed Learning Outcome (SOLO) taxonomy, a method of classifying learning outcomes in terms of their complexity as learning progresses, based on five levels: (1) prestructural, (2) unistructural, (3) multistructural, (4) relational, and (5) extended abstract. This allows teachers to assess students' work in terms of its quality and not simply by a right-or-wrong dichotomy. As teachers work to manage behavior in the classroom by creating a positive learning environment, they can guide students' work through these stages to learn the process of self-regulation.

Prior to learning, few, if any, students would have knowledge of the concept the teacher wants them to explore. During the prestructural phase, students may be resistant to trying, may demonstrate incorrect procedure or work output, or may ask the teacher for greater assistance. Then, students enter what Nottingham (n.d.) refers to as the *learning pit*. At the outset of learning, students may hit on only one or two aspects of a task (unistructural) before progressing to several aspects but not yet connecting them (multistructural), then beginning to integrate them into a whole (relational), and finally gaining the ability to generalize that whole to future, untaught applications (extended abstract). Nottingham's (n.d.) four stages flow as follows:

1. **Concept:** The Learning Challenge begins with a concept. The concept can come from the teacher instruction, conversation, observations, something students heard or saw in the media or the curriculum. So long as students have at least some understanding of the concept then the Learning Challenge can work. In SOLO Taxonomy terms, this is the *uni-structural* stage.

2. **Conflict:** The key to the Learning Challenge is to get students "into the pit" by creating cognitive conflict in their minds. This deliberate creation of a dilemma is what makes the Learning Challenge such a good model for challenge and inquiry. It is also the frequent experience of cognitive conflict that helps build a growth mindset (Dweck, 2006). . . . As for the SOLO Taxonomy, stage 2 represents the *multi-structural* stage.

3. **Construct:** After a while of being "in the pit," students begin to construct meaning for themselves. They do this by identifying relationships, explaining causes and integrating ideas into a new structure. As they do this, they experience a sense of "eureka" in which they have a new sense of clarity. This in turn puts them in an ideal position to help those students who are still confused. In SOLO Taxonomy terms, this is when students move to the *relational* stage of understanding.

4. **Consider:** Once "out of the pit," students should be encouraged to reflect on the stages of thinking they've just been through—from a single, simplistic idea (stage 1) to the identification of . . . conflicting, ideas [or potential solutions] (stage 2) right through to a new understanding of more complex and inter-related ideas (stage 3). They should then look for ways to relate and apply their new understanding to different contexts. In SOLO Taxonomy terms, this is the *extended abstract* stage of hypothesis, generalisation and application to new contexts.

Figure 4.1 (pages 52–53) illustrates this process.

Building opportunities for students to succeed in class early in their academics also helps them build essential behavioral skills. Although the term *discipline* has taken on a negative tone, discipline is not actually something we do to students; it is something we help students attain. It means turning disruptions into learning opportunities so that disruptive students learn responsible and respectful ways to meet their needs both in school and beyond school. Having structures in place to improve the culture of your classroom has significant benefits toward supporting and responding to student behavior. The remainder of this chapter will offer tools and strategies to support teachers as they build these structures and shape the positive learning environments in their classrooms to produce the behaviors students must learn for success in school and life.

Strategies and Tools for Fostering Positive Behaviors

There are a myriad of tools available for teachers to build positive learning environments and develop the desired behaviors (and school successes) for all students. This section offers two tools to assist teachers in gathering data to get to the root of why problem behaviors are occurring with individual students, and strategies teachers can use to respond to those behaviors and support positive behaviors for all students in the class.

ABC: An Early Analysis Tool

An earlier version of this strategy originally appeared in Hierck, 2017.

ABC is a direct-observation tool that teachers can use to collect information about why a student is not demonstrating proficiency for a behavior. The *A* refers to the antecedent (the event, activity, or environment) immediately before the problem behavior. The *B* refers to the behavior the teacher observes, and the *C* refers to the consequence the teacher imposes for the behavior. To assist in this evidence gathering, the teacher can complete a simple chart like figure 4.2 (page 54) as he or she develops a potential intervention strategy. See page 62 for a free reproducible version of this figure.

Let's look at an example. The teacher calls on Charlie to be the first reader in class. Charlie says he'd rather not read, slams his book shut, and throws it off his desk. The teacher then sends Charlie to the hallway, but he decides to head to the office. In this case, the antecedent (A) is the request made by the teacher. Let's be clear; this is a reasonable, typical request in a classroom environment. So what might be causing such an overt response? Perhaps Charlie is a poor reader and does not want this exposed to his peers. Perhaps he is shy and uncomfortable with public speaking. Perhaps it is the time of day when he is not school ready. Charlie's behavior (B) is to disagree, slam his book shut, and throw his book off the desk. Remember, all behavior occurs

JAMES NOTTINGHAM'S
THE LEARNING CHALLENGE

Easy Learning

Deep Learning

Concept
Find a concept worth exploring that you know a little bit about.

The Pit

Question
Find the problems, the nuances and the exceptions to your concept. You can do this by comparing your concept with another, considering if it always applies, or trying to find a definition that works in all cases.

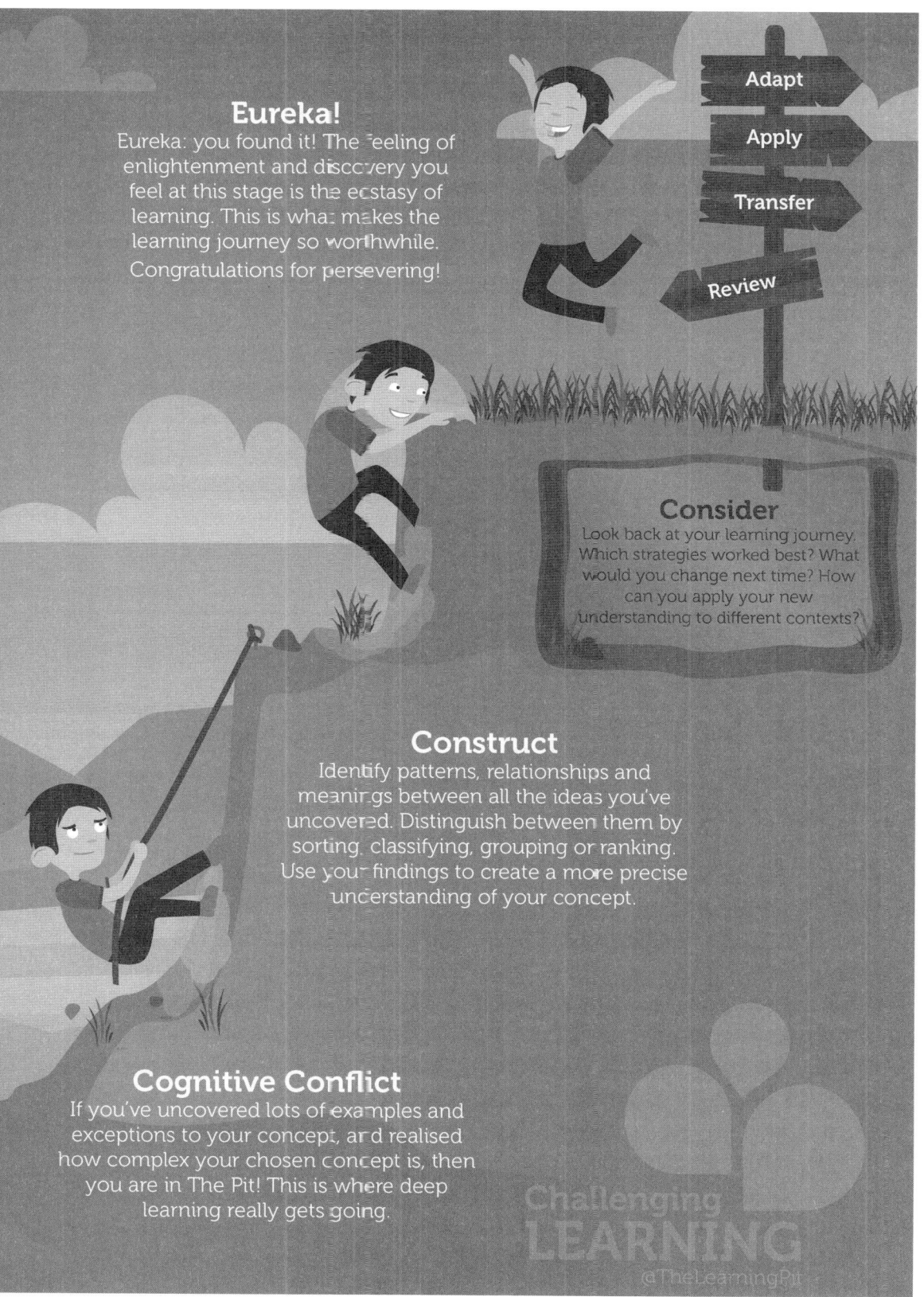

Source: © 2018 by Challenging Learning. Used with permission.

Figure 4.1: The Learning Challenge.

Date	Time	Antecedent	Behavior	Consequence	Possible Function (Why is this behavior occurring?)

Source: Hierck, 2017, p. 68.

Figure 4.2: The ABC direct-observation tool.

Visit **go.SolutionTree.com/behavior** *for a free reproducible version of this figure.*

for one of two reasons: to get something or to avoid something. His consequence (C) is removal from class. The teacher needs to ask herself this question: "Is this consequence having the desired effect?" If it is not (that is, if the misbehavior still occurs regularly), then the teacher must have a next step to pursue. In this case, the *function* of Charlie's behavior is to escape the classroom and avoid the request. There is another way to process this challenge while ensuring the success of the long-term objective (oral reading) and closing Charlie's behavioral gap.

In this scenario, the teacher asks Charlie to perform a reasonable task. Let's assume this is not the first time the teacher has seen Charlie's response (that is, the teacher is prepared with baseline data). The teacher should build an appropriate intervention plan from there. She may have noticed that Charlie performs better when he receives some early warning about the upcoming tasks. In this example, the response might be to pick the section and allow Charlie to practice in advance. If the challenge relates to some other environmental concern (time of day or day of the week, for example), the teacher can structure a similar approach. If Charlie's response remains the same following these interventions, the teacher could engage in an alternative response that does not result in removal or task avoidance. For example, a quiet zone within the classroom could be created. Think about how much time a student misses in high-quality instruction and engagement when the teacher sends the student out of the room. Often, these are students who already have considerable gaps in their learning and need more instructional time. Perhaps the student could use a signal card system (see in chapter 5, page 77). Charlie could let the teacher know when he is green (good to go), yellow (starting to slow), or red (ready to blow) before acting out. The use of an alternative learning environment (a colleague's classroom or a quiet space in the classroom) could also help Charlie, and avoid involving the office. These interventions require context, and the responses will vary from student to student. However, the ultimate goal remains the same—helping Charlie close the gaps in his learning, both academic and behavioral.

Problem Behavior Questionnaire

Another tool I have found beneficial to use is a tool crafted by associate professor of special education Timothy J. Lewis, assistant professor of special education Terrance M. Scott, and professor of special education George Sugai (1994) called a *problem behavior questionnaire* (figure 4.3, page 56). This questionnaire allows teachers to home in on significant antecedents (such as time of day, activity, or other students) to students' negative behaviors.

Once teachers have determined the cause of negative behavior, they can begin to explore potential solutions. The strategies offered in the next section are designed to support these solutions to create the desired behaviors.

Behavior Support Strategies

There are many strategies that teachers can use to plan, implement, and evaluate structures for fostering positive behaviors. The following list includes ways to set classroom expectations, practice positive reinforcement, and employ differentiation and enrichment tools that build positive classroom structures. As you plan your activities and set measurable and achievable goals, these strategies will help you create a positive learning environment in your classroom.

DNA Activities

Tap into what motivates students and what students bring to the classroom by discovering their desires, needs, and assets (DNA). This is best done at the start of the school year but should not wait if that opportunity was missed. Engaging in activities that connect students to each other and to their teacher is never a bad strategy. The more teachers know about their students, the more they see students beyond their proficiency levels on a specific learning target. The more students know about their teachers, the more they see them as more than educators. Here are a couple of activities you might try.

- **Me Bag:** Provide a large bag (like a grocery bag) in which a student can place items that relate to him- or herself in some way. As each item is removed, the student explains to his or her classmates the personal connection. The teacher may consider modeling this first using his or her own items.

Problem Behavior Questionnaire

Student _____ Grade _____

Teacher _____ Date _____

Specific Behavior Description

_____

Directions: Focus on a typical episode of problem behavior; circle the frequency at which each of the following statements is true.

	Never	10%	25%	50%	75%	90%	Always
1. Does the problem behavior occur and persist when you make a request to perform a task?	0	1	2	3	4	5	6
2. When the problem behavior occurs do you redirect the student to get back to task or follow rules?	0	1	2	3	4	5	6
3. During a conflict with peers, if the student engages in the problem behavior do peers leave the student alone?	0	1	2	3	4	5	6
4. When the problem behavior occurs do peers verbally respond or laugh at the student?	0	1	2	3	4	5	6
5. Is the problem behavior more likely to occur following a conflict outside the classroom (e.g., bus write-up)?	0	1	2	3	4	5	6
6. Does the problem behavior occur to get your attention when you are working with other students?	0	1	2	3	4	5	6
7. Does the problem behavior occur in the presence of specific peers?	0	1	2	3	4	5	6
8. Is the problem behavior more likely to continue to occur throughout the day following an earlier episode?	0	1	2	3	4	5	6

Source: Lewis et al., 1994. Used with permission.

Figure 4.3: Problem behavior questionnaire.

- **Icebreaker:** Get (or create) small stones that each have one word (like *happiness*, *friendship*, or *growth*) etched into them, and place them in a cooler full of ice cubes (or any other method that is practical for the teacher). Have students "break the ice" and remove the stones. In small groups, pass around a stone, and have each student describe how the word on the stone connects to him or her.

Check-In Check-Out (CICO)

This strategy is a research-based monitoring and mentoring tool that can support students as they build better habits, including self-monitoring behavior, by identifying the behaviors that are getting in the way of learning and reflecting on progress toward correcting those behaviors. I suggest starting with two behaviors, allowing the teacher and the student to each identify one. This builds awareness and also helps the student to begin the process of self-regulating. Students and teachers can use a CICO form (see figure 4.4) to reflect and track progress on these behaviors. See page 63 for a free reproducible version of this figure. Depending on the school schedule, they can complete the columns in the form by period or by time of day. Both the teacher and the student assign a value for the behavior during the identified time frame.

CICO for _____

Check-In Check-Out with Ms./Mr. _____ Date: _____

Today I am working on _____.

This is how I did today.

3 = Great! (I was reminded to _____ 1 or 0 times.)

2 = Pretty good (I was reminded to _____ 3 or 2 times.)

1 = Not yet (I was reminded to _____ more than 3 times.)

Behavior:

Times of Day	Teacher	Student

Today I earned _____ points.

Figure 4.4: CICO form.

*Visit **go.SolutionTree.com/behavior** for a free reproducible version of this figure.*

The key to CICO is to have an adult who has a commitment to building positive, effective relationships with the students—not someone who is looking for misbehavior as a way to accelerate consequences or labeling. The objective is to show growth toward more positive, productive behaviors with less time lost to negative behaviors and recognize growth as it occurs. If a student is struggling consistently with behavior—for example, he or she is scoring 1s—it is important to notice the periods or time when scores move up. Establishing a reasonable goal with the student (perhaps a weekly points target, for example) may increase the effectiveness of this tool.

Class Meetings

This proactive strategy sets aside time for students to discuss classroom issues as a group. Class meetings can yield significant behavioral benefits, such as helping set the tone for respectful learning, establishing a climate of trust, developing empathy, and encouraging collaboration. It's important to recognize these meetings may need to occur outside a prescribed, scheduled time. If you notice other issues preventing students from responding positively to your instruction, you may need to have a time-out from the instruction to address the issue.

Daily Tasks and Routines

Establishing daily tasks and routines supports students in knowing the teacher's expectations from the moment they arrive in the classroom. Get in the habit of having a regular structure to your class, and stick to it. Students who struggle to maintain appropriate behaviors do not respond well to off-the-cuff modifications to their day. Keep challenging tasks to the early part of the day (prior to lunch).

Practice, Review, and Model Expectations

As teachers determine strategies for managing their classrooms, they should practice them early on, review their expectations, and model those expectations for students. Explicit instruction followed by modeling of the desired behaviors is important for students who may not be familiar with those behaviors. Do not assume they have learned them elsewhere.

Two-by-Ten

This strategy allows for a student and teacher to build a connection that might not have existed previously. Spend two minutes per day for ten consecutive days talking with an at-risk student about anything he or she wants to talk about. This may yield unique interests (or common ones with the adult!) or some background that may help explain some of the behaviors a student exhibits. The key is to allow the student to drive the talk, as this allows the student to see that the teacher is interested in him or her beyond the academic content or classwork. This helps build a positive

Supporting a Positive Learning Environment

relationship based on interests the student has and is willing to share and reveals an adult who is caring beyond pedagogy.

STORY

This strategy, devised by Greg Wolcott, assistant superintendent for teaching and learning in Woodridge, Illinois, helps teachers know each student's strengths, talents, opportunities for growth, resources, and yearnings (STORY; G. Wolcott, personal communication, August 2016). Figure 4.5 provides an example of a student's STORY and how the teacher gained and used this information to support the student.

- **Strengths:** Ms. Morrison spent time the first three days getting to know all of her students. She started by administering the VIA Institute on Character (www.viacharacter.org) strengths inventory and found out that Maddie's top strengths were in the areas of love, kindness, and leadership.

- **Talents:** Next, Ms. Morrison became a student of her students by watching for their individual tendencies throughout the school day. She noticed that Maddie was always happy and energetic, had great oral language abilities, and always walked her brother to his classroom.

- **Opportunities for growth:** Having closely observed Maddie, Ms. Morrison took note that Maddie suffered from a lack of persistence, frequently giving up on activities when they became overly challenging, and not tackling difficult tasks. This included reading books at challenging levels.

- **Resources:** Based on surveys sent home and meeting Maddie's parents, Ms. Morrison learned that Maddie had many resources at her disposal. Both parents were actively involved in her learning, and she didn't lack for food, attention, or love (some of Maslow's basic needs) on a daily basis.

- **Yearnings:** Ms. Morrison spent several minutes talking with Maddie about her love of learning and her passions and goals. She quickly learned that Maddie wanted to be a teacher when she grew up.

Based on the data collected and anecdotal information, Ms. Morrison felt she had a good understanding of Maddie and her STORY. Ms. Morrison then went to work developing a peer-tutoring program that would allow Maddie the opportunity to begin reading more challenging books followed by teaching and retelling them to younger female students. By utilizing Maddie's oral language strengths, her passion for teaching others, and her leadership skills, Ms. Morrison was able to develop an effective way to increase the level and difficulty of the texts Maddie read while leveraging some of Maddie's identified strengths. Within weeks, Maddie had increased not only her reading level but also her persistence, which helped her become a more confident student, ready to tackle the challenges she faced.

Source: Hierck, 2017, p. 50.

Figure 4.5: Maddie's STORY.

Three-to-One Praise Ratio

Building a positive learning community requires an emphasis on authentic, meaningful, and personalized praise that engages students in their growth. Psychology professor Barbara L. Fredrickson's (2013) research identifies that a ratio of three to one (3:1) typically serves as the tipping point at which an individual will flourish (including having resilience to hard times) rather than languish. A 3:1 ratio of identifying, noticing, and chronicling positive to negative behavior translates into 75 percent positive behavior. Some educators have also identified the ratio as higher. The number is not as important as the actions. In my personal experience, it is not as easy to achieve this ratio as it may seem. If you have difficulty, I suggest trying what I did: begin with a goal to achieve a balance (1:1) as your first step, and then intentionally focus on noticing the positives much more than identifying the negatives. What you look for, you will see.

Direct to Correct to Connect

The direct to correct to connect strategy allows teachers to clearly distinguish how they respond to unwanted behavior on a continuum from negative consequences to positive outcomes. It encourages a shift that moves away from the direct approach often seen in older approaches to education, toward the positive outcomes the connect approach achieves.

- The *direct* approach sounds like an order, such as "Stop interrupting class!" and is followed by a consequence.
- The *correct* approach implies an attempt to remediate, such as "Raise your hand before talking," and is still followed by a consequence.
- The *connect* approach is the action the teacher takes to remind the student of the key expectation (for example, respect) and how the student should follow this, such as "In our respectful environment, we raise our hands when we have a thought to share." While a consequence may still occur, it is paired with an instructional opportunity.

Yet

This strategy encourages teachers to focus on the word *yet*. Recognizing that students have not achieved the desired outcome *yet* indicates there is still the possibility for them to achieve their goal and teachers are committed to helping them achieve it. Teachers need to practice using this word in situations where a student experiences frustration and is ready to give up. A continued reminder that growth is still possible may be enough to encourage students to achieve that growth.

When teachers can identify the root of students' inappropriate behaviors and respond to students' needs using the strategies described here, they create the positive learning environments students need to excel in both behavioral and academic goals.

The Takeaways

This chapter has emphasized the importance of maintaining a positive approach and seeking out strategies to further this approach when creating learning environments that are conducive to managing student behavior. The key ideas from this chapter include the following.

- Being positive by design is a conscious decision educators make to notice and recognize student behaviors that align with the stated expectations. It is about choice.

- Best practice and the practice you are best at might not be the same thing. Look at the evidence to see what has the greatest impact.

- Nothing happens by chance in a successful learning environment.

- The learning pit allows for productive struggle and eventual growth in academics and behavior.

- Students learn appropriate behaviors the same way they learn academics—through instruction, practice, feedback, and encouragement.

- It's important for educators to have some tools or strategies to create desired behaviors.

Before moving on to the next chapter, please reflect on the following questions: What proactive initiatives that promote a positive learning environment exist in your classroom and school? What tools and strategies from this chapter might you use to support such an environment?

The ABC Direct-Observation Tool

Date	Time	Antecedent	Behavior	Consequence	Possible Function (Why is this behavior occurring?)

Source: Hierck, T. (2017). Seven keys to a positive learning environment in your classroom. Bloomington, IN: Solution Tree Press.

Managing Unstoppable Learning © 2019 Solution Tree Press • SolutionTree.com
Visit **go.SolutionTree.com/behavior** to download this free reproducible.

CICO Form

CICO for _____

Check-In Check-Out with Ms./Mr. _____ Date: _____

Today I am working on _____.

This is how I did today.

3 = Great! (I was reminded to _____ 1 or 0 times.)

2 = Pretty good (I was reminded to _____ 3 or 2 times.)

1 = Not yet (I was reminded to _____ more than 3 times.)

Behavior:		
Times of Day	**Teacher**	**Student**

Today I earned _____ points.

Managing Unstoppable Learning © 2019 Solution Tree Press • SolutionTree.com
Visit **go.SolutionTree.com/behavior** to download this free reproducible.

CHAPTER 5

RESPONDING TO PROBLEM BEHAVIORS

There is a choice you have to make in everything you do. So keep in mind that in the end, the choice you make, makes you.

—John Wooden

Let me begin this chapter with a confession—as an educator, I didn't always get it right when I responded to misbehavior. I had times when my energy level and my decision making were not the best, and I assigned responsibility for all the necessary change to the student. I can also recall that, more often than not, I left such exchanges with a gnawing in the pit of my stomach. For the student, I was likely just another adult in a long line of adults who let him or her down and who behaved the way he or she had come to expect adults to behave when he or she struggled. I suspect I am not alone in this lament as an educator, but the reality is none of us gets to have a do-over. However, fresh opportunities lie in front of us, and we can use the learning from those past missed opportunities to fashion the right steps going forward.

Let me also clearly state that we will never eliminate problem behavior. To those who suggest the solution is to remove students who display inappropriate behavior or to set them up in separate classrooms or schools, I offer what I call the *tissue box theory* of student behavior. Removing problem behavior students is akin to pulling a fresh tissue from the box. Once you pull up one, another one quickly pops up, as it's not the end of the supply. If you remove the worst problem behavior in your classroom, the problem won't go away, as another student will occupy the vacancy. The solution that will change what they exhibit as students lies in changing what we do as adults. In our teaching profession, the focus has always been on ensuring academic progress for all students. This is a laudable goal, and it must remain part of the ongoing work of schools. But equally important will be a focus on behavioral and social targets. In this chapter, we will first take a look at the *why*—or motivations—of behavior, and then examine teachers' responsibility when it comes to management of problem behaviors. Next, we'll explore the concept of defiance and ways to respond when defiant students act out. We'll then consider how to approach behavioral interventions with students in our classrooms. Finally, the chapter will offer ideas for how teachers can develop and prioritize academic and social behavior targets to accompany their learning targets.

The Why of Behavior

What first thought comes to mind when you see the word *behavior*? Is it a negative image or notion? All of us engage in behavior every day, all day. Behavior is driven by one of two motivators: (1) to get something or (2) to avoid something (Cooper, Heron, & Heward, 2007).

Think about your personal behavior outside of school, for example. Does it change based on how badly you want something or how much you'd like to avoid a task? I can recall many occasions where my desire for task avoidance meant I found something else *incredibly urgent* (note the sarcasm) to tend to. Think about all your behaviors today. Did you try to avoid something or gain something? Did your efforts to do either of these result in your exerting power or control? This is the *why* of behavior, and it's not markedly different for students.

Behavior is a communicative device, and sometimes educators need to take a step back to ensure they hear the message. When a student exhibits behavior contrary to the established routines, he or she communicates, albeit in a way counterproductive to a positive learning environment, a personal struggle or challenge. When teachers establish classroom routines and procedures, it is a well-intended attempt to control students' behavior—their communication—and the learning environment. Teachers have an opportunity to improve the level of sophistication in this communication through teaching.

Educators' Responsibility

If it's not educators' responsibility to teach the appropriate social behaviors that students must display while at school, or to teach the desired academic behaviors that will enable them to learn how to learn, then whose responsibility is it? It would be folly to expect parents to teach their children how to behave at school both socially and academically, as they don't live and work in our world. The fact that schools have chosen to not explicitly define, teach, reinforce, and remediate behaviors in the past does not mean they should not do so now. When educators talk about teaching the skills necessary to succeed in life beyond graduation, it's never been as critical, for our students and our societies, that they embrace this responsibility and see it as a cherished opportunity. School staff active participation in identifying what they value most in the behavioral realm requires a higher level of professionalism and sense of urgency than just focusing on cooperation and good manners. If we really believe that all students can learn, then we will spend our time and effort on our adult actions and behaviors that make this a reality for all students, not by lowering our standards but by elevating all students to reach them and by collaboratively planning interventions that will help students close the gap.

Fisher and Frey (2015) talk about the importance of adults taking ownership of this challenge:

> There is a strong correlation between a teacher's sense of efficacy of classroom management and how successfully he or she is able to manage problematic behavior. . . . In other words, a teacher with fewer skills regarding behavior management impacts the student's behavior and the larger school environment. (p. 138)

The good news is that we know what works; we have many colleagues reaping the benefits of effective practice, and we can take a collective approach that will improve the skill set of all educators in this area of problem behaviors.

Here's the reality—I don't know where else in the life of a child (and in his or her subsequent adult life) a better collection of talented individuals will gather to ameliorate the negative behaviors he or she exhibits. The skills that exist in the educator population in any school, when coalesced around a common goal, are too great to allow for anything other than a positive resolution. Identifying and teaching academic and behavior priority standards are critical to achieving this positive outcome.

Academic and Social Behavior Priority Standards

In order to teach expected academic and social behaviors, it's important that teachers first clearly identify those behaviors and skills they want to see from their students. *Academic behaviors* are anything a student does that helps him or her do well in school. These could include applying study habits, taking notes, or paying attention in class, for example. *Social behaviors* are the interactions among individuals—your students—that allow them to fully participate in classroom experiences. Just as teachers have done with academic standards, it makes sense to establish the priority standards in these domains also.

Academic Behaviors

Academic behaviors describe a set of cognitive skills that are integral to success in school and life. They guide the *how* of meeting expectations for student success. These are sometimes described as *self-regulatory strategies* or *executive functioning skills* and are part of the skills all students will need for their lives after high school. Table 5.1 lists examples of standards and learning targets for desirable behaviors for teachers to consider supporting through instruction.

Table 5.1: Prioritizing Academic Behaviors

Standard	Learning Target
Metacognitive Practices	Knowledge and beliefs about thinking
Self-Concept	Seeing oneself as smart
Self-Monitoring	Ability to plan and prepare
Engagement	Ability to maintain interest
Volition	Efforts needed to stay motivated
Emotional Control	Techniques for regulating response to situations

Source: Hierck & Weber, 2014, p. 21.

Social Behaviors

Social behaviors are important in their own right for students to master to become productive, contributing citizens in their various communities. Students with challenges in the social behavior domain will have difficulties learning academic skills, either because their behaviors distract them from fully participating in classroom experiences or because their behaviors remove them from the classroom due to visits to the office or suspensions. The results of a major international study from the Organisation for Economic Co-operation and Development (OECD, 2017) support teaching social learning targets. This triennial international survey aims to evaluate education systems worldwide by testing the skills and knowledge of fifteen-year-old students in science, mathematics, and reading. In 2015, the study also examined collaborative problem solving, and the results indicate much higher levels of success in this domain for U.S. students than in the others. However, Andreas Schleicher, who oversees the PISA tests the OECD reported on, wrote in an editorial note accompanying the PISA score report:

> As workplaces around the globe are demanding—and paying higher wages for—people with well-honed social skills, schools need to do more to help their students develop these skills. . . . Strong academic skills will not automatically also lead to strong social skills. (OECD, 2017, pp. 3, 7)

While students scored well in collaborative skills, this does not automatically translate to strong social skills. We must intentionally develop these skills in our students. The same intentional focus that is part of academic success planning will need to be comparable for behavioral success. Cassetta and Sawyer (2013) remind educators,

"Just as we know that students don't enter our classrooms having mastered all of the academic standards, students also require our assistance in becoming socially and emotionally competent" (p. 20). Social behaviors are also critical because of their interconnectedness with academics. Collaboration and cooperation are especially significant.

Defiance

More often than not, when I work in schools and the conversation turns to the most challenging student behaviors that need to be dealt with, a catchall category emerges: *defiance*. Let's define this as challenges to the power and authority of the teacher. According to a report on suspensions in California schools, in 2012–2013, 34 percent of out-of-school suspensions were for defiance or disruption (Losen, Martinez, & Okelola, 2014).

The debate about how to deal with student defiance becomes even more polarizing than the issue itself. In a report on suspension trends in California, Daniel J. Losen, Michael A. Keith, Cheri L. Hodson, Tia E. Martinez, and Shakti Belway (2015) identify two schools of thought on the issue. One camp includes those who "believe the high number of suspensions is causing students to lose class time" (Losen et al., 2015, p. ii) and increasing students' risk for dropping out and, ultimately, becoming part of the juvenile justice system. The second camp has the "concern that the educational environment will suffer if schools reduce their use of suspension" and allow "those kids" to remain in class (Losen et al., 2015, p. ii). Regardless of perspective, students who struggle clearly need more time in class, not less. After the state of California took measures to address the disparate nature of suspensions for willful defiance—including re-examining what constituted defiance, considering what supports were necessary to enable restorative practices, and training teachers on building a positive climate that engages students in learning—school suspension rates decreased. (Please note the state still has considerable work to do in this area according to Losen et al. [2015].) This outcome is not surprising, as educators know from experience that focused initiatives on a single topic tend to have immediate impact. Moving beyond this Hawthorne effect (the notion that behavior changes simply because we know someone is observing us), the authors draw this very significant conclusion:

> Some readers may think curtailing suspensions would have a negative impact, but this report starts and ends with examples that counter the assumption that frequent suspensions are necessary to protect the learning environment. *Specifically, the introductory statewide analysis shows that, in California, lower district suspension rates are correlated with higher district achievement.* (Losen et al., 2015, p. ii)

While I'm not suggesting defiance shouldn't concern teachers, it is how teachers react to defiant behavior in the classroom that will lead to reductions in consequences and a greater focus on learning—not removing students from class for defiant behavior. This really is about improving the learning environment. I've come to understand from my years of personal experience working in schools that when students behave defiantly, a desire to feel relevant in the classroom usually drives their defiance. Correspondingly, the adult often has the same desire. Left unchecked, this scenario turns into a power struggle. These struggles happen because teachers may feel like students are testing them (which they oftentimes are) and teachers get angry or irritated. However, teachers never win power struggles. Once the escalation begins, you have lost, not only with the target student but also with the rest of the class. Any attempt to return to teaching after the escalation is difficult, as the adrenaline is still running through you and is heightened in many students. Here's the reality: *no one* wins a power struggle. So teachers must find more effective responses to defiance.

Responses to Defiance

So what's the best way to avoid a power struggle and help a defiant student? How might teachers manage their classrooms and continue to move the learning agenda forward? I believe developing a clear definition of *classroom management* is a good starting point, and I favor (as do Smith et al., 2015) one that Cassetta and Sawyer (2013) offer. They define classroom management as "building relationships with students and teaching social skills along with academic skills" (p. 16). Of the many strategies that exist for approaching this work, I find these three especially helpful: (1) address the student's needs, (2) pair consequences with instruction, and (3) teach resilience.

Address the Student's Needs

When a student behaves defiantly, begin by calmly working with the student, and find ways to address his or her genuine need to feel significant. This does not mean lowering the bar or having different expectations for some students. It's important to demonstrate that you still hold the student (and all the other students) accountable for meeting expectations.

As Spencer Kagan, Patricia Kyle, and Sally Scott (2004) state, "We never accept student disruption, but we will always validate the child's position" (p. 160). Developing responsible ways to meet the needs students communicate via their negative behavior is crucial in teaching students responsible thinking and behaviors. For example, if a student lacks positive communication skills and grows up in an environment where curse words are routine, don't be surprised when he or she uses those words when he or she gets frustrated or disagrees with a routine. Also realize that the flagrant use of that inappropriate language guarantees attention and a response. As Fisher and Frey (2015) note, "The truth is that we all seek the most efficient behavior that will communicate what we want" (p. 139). As we work with students to build their skills, we must focus on adding more tools to their toolbox. There's an old adage that if the only tool you have in your toolbox is a hammer, everything looks like a nail. If students lack the verbal skills to communicate positively, they will communicate negatively, unless they learn the skills to communicate otherwise. This may mean, for example, helping the student to become aware of his or her use of curse words. Early on in my career, I had the opportunity to work with students labeled as having severe behavior challenges. The use of curse words was often the norm, and my classroom might have been empty before lunch each day if I had just resorted to giving a consequence of removal (as per the general school policy at the time) each time an offensive word was uttered. It became apparent that often the words were used not in anger, but out of familiarity. I took to recording my interactions with students to share with them how often they used particular words. They were surprised as well (validating for me that it was not always an angry exchange), and we used that realization to think about other, more positive words that could be inserted instead of the curse word. This helped to build vocabulary skills as well as self-regulating skills.

Teachers can also be proactive in helping the student avoid defiant behavior in the first place. Consider the following list of recommendations from Hierck and Weber (2014):

- Praise, but use caution when praising defiant students. Do not embarrass. Ensure praise is sincere, specific, and not embarrassing. Deliver praise as soon as possible. . . .
- Keep responses calm, brief, and businesslike. Sarcasm and lengthy negative reprimands can trigger defiant student behavior. Instead, respond in a neutral, businesslike, calm voice. Brief responses prevent staff from inadvertently rewarding misbehaving students with attention.
- Listen actively. Project a sincere desire to understand and summarize student concerns. . . .
- Help avoid a full-blown conflict by allowing the student to save face; students sometimes blunder into potential confrontations. Ask the student, "Is there anything that we can work out together so that you can stay in the classroom and be successful?" Treat the student with dignity, model negotiation and conflict resolution skills, and demonstrate that adults respect and value students. It provides the student with a final chance to resolve the conflict and avoid more serious consequences. Students may initially give a sarcastic or unrealistic response (e.g., "Yeah, you can leave me alone and stop trying to get me to do classwork!"). Ignore such power struggles and simply ask again whether there is a reasonable way to engage the student's cooperation. . . .

- Proactively intervene. Staff may interrupt escalating behaviors by redirecting student attention. If defiant behavior is just beginning, engage the student in a high-interest activity, such as playing an educational computer game or helping in the classroom. Or, remove the student from the room to prevent escalation; send the student on an errand to provide time to calm down.
- Project calmness. Staff must control their own behavior when attempting to defuse a confrontation with a defiant student. Approach the student at a slow, deliberate pace and maintain a reasonable distance. . . . Avoid staring, hands on hips, or finger pointing. . . .
- Give positive choices. When a student's disrespect indicates a need for control, structure requests to acknowledge the freedom to choose whether to comply or receive a logical consequence. Frame requests as a two-part statement. First, present the negative choice and its consequences, then state the positive behavioral choice that staff would like the student to select. . . .
- Identify a corner of the room (or area outside the classroom with adult supervision) where students can take a brief break. Make breaks available to all students. When a student becomes upset and defiant, offer to talk the situation over once he or she has calmed down and then direct the student to the cool-down corner.
- Ask neutral, open-ended questions to collect more information before responding when faced with a confrontational student. Pose who, what, where, when, and how questions to more fully understand the problem situation and identify possible solutions. Avoid asking why questions because they can imply that you are blaming the student. (pp. 136–137)

These strategies promote social respect, minimize defiance, and provide alternative approaches to what may cause escalation.

Pair Consequences With Instruction

Consequences are generally thought of as results of a particular action or situation, and both students and adults often regard them as bad or inconvenient. When delivered from a power position, they don't tend to result in much change. When it comes to consequences, remember that change won't happen through consequence alone. Change happens when consequence is paired with instruction. Also, what the teacher might think of as a consequence could, in fact, reinforce the negative behavior. Removal from class might not seem like a bad option to a student who knows he or she struggles in that content area (and the student might perceive embarrassing the teacher in the process as an added bonus if it allows the student to save face in front of his or her peers). The reality is that the gap he or she has in the content area will only grow as he or she misses more brilliant teaching.

Additionally, psychologist Anita Woolfolk Hoy and professor of education Carol S. Weinstein (2006) state, "Such attempts to hold students publicly accountable for their behavior can render them compliant but can also make them feel anger, humiliation, and a range of other negative emotions that serve to shut down learning" (p. 183). I have yet to meet a student who got "consequenced" to better behavior. A teacher who implements a consequence may win the minor skirmish, but the long-term impact of a consequence in isolation may result in a fractured relationship from which neither side might recover. Smith et al. (2015) indicate:

> Students who are punished will come up with a list of reasons why they are the victims and will channel their negative emotion toward those doing the punishing. Instead of reflecting on their behavior or making amends, they will plot how to avoid detection the next time. (p. 9)

This suggests students who are punished will focus more energy on revenge than on change, taking the form of intentionally hurting another's things, hurting other people, or damaging property. They also tend to learn the wrong life lesson. As Smith et al. (2015) note, "Most troubling of all, punished children learn from adult examples that exerting power is the way for them to get what they want—a notion diametrically opposed to the social and emotional well-being we are trying to foster" (p. 9). When students are younger (in the early elementary grades), adults may intimidate them into complying. The power imbalance favors the adult. But as they grow, the perception of power shifts, and students behave in a fashion that challenges authority or questions the arbitrary nature of rules (Hierck, 2017; refer back to the section in chapter 2 titled Expectations, Not Rules [page 22]). They grow up with the notion of "might is right."

I am not suggesting schools should eliminate any notion of consequence, as this would not be practical. I am suggesting in order to have impact, you must always pair consequence with instruction. If we never teach students the desired behaviors, why would we expect them to demonstrate those behaviors? If we respond by simply taking things away (for example, think about the arbitrary nature of penalty points for missing deadlines) to improve behavior, we run the risk of the exact opposite occurring. As an educator, how would you respond if your district took out 20 percent of your next paycheck because you did not submit your report card grades on time? When I posed that question to a large audience at a conference, I received predictably negative answers. Colleagues indicated that they would no longer want to work as hard, that it would impact their relationship with the district, or that they would find a way to retaliate for the district taking what they believed to be theirs. Why would we expect our students to respond any differently?

Teach Resilience

Let's examine a skill that I consider critical for all students—resilience. Psychologist Donald Meichenbaum (n.d.) describes *resilience* as "the ability to show positive adaptation in spite of significant life adversities and the ability to adapt to difficult and challenging life experiences." This poses the capacity for resilience to replace defiant behaviors with more positive ones. Meichenbaum (n.d.) explains, "Resilient individuals can get distressed, but they are able to manage the negative behavioral outcomes in the face of risks without becoming debilitated." Further, as educators Laura Lippman and Hanna Schmitz (2013) state, "Numerous studies show that programs and practices that build resilience are particularly effective in improving the academic performance of low achieving students." It is possible to teach resilience, and the following list from Hierck and Weber (2014) provide suggestions for how teachers might structure this important work:

- Explicitly teach and model coping skills.
- Guide students in using a visual or written "Rating the intensity of emotions" guide to label and appropriately manage their feelings.
- Teach, model, and practice self-talk scripts.
  - The staff member and the student create a script that defines thoughts, words, and actions that the student can follow in target situations.
  - Use of the script is first practiced with the student, and can be followed verbatim by the student during the first few uses.
  - Use of the explicit script is faded as behaviors improve.
  - The staff member checks in with the student regularly to reinforce, remind, and reteach.
- Assign journaling and promote the practice as a healthy reflective tool.
- Ensure that students know how to access adults, and which adults to access.
- Prepare an "emotional-plan" with students. Role-play different situations and how students should emotionally respond.
- Encourage students to reward themselves for dealing with difficult situations well.
- Teach relaxation techniques:
  - Deep Breathing
  - Count to 10
  - Draw
  - Color
  - Scribble
  - Read
  - Visualization
  - Listen to music or nature sounds
  - Take a break (pp. 149–150)

In the absence of instruction for those students who challenge the most, there is limited potential for change. Those students (and their families) who challenge you the most need you the most.

Intervention: When and If

Throughout this book, I emphasize that all students need to remain in class with the experts (their teachers) all the time so that the learning opportunities are maximized. I also want to ensure that teaching occurs for behavioral outcomes as it does for academic ones. I further recognize there comes a time where the teacher needs to make a decision as to the immediacy of the intervention, as some might be part of a longer-term remediation. Professor of education Herbert Grossman (2004) provides four key questions for teachers to consider when deciding next steps.

1. **Is the behavior harmful?** If the behavior poses an immediate risk to personal safety, you will need to intervene.

2. **Is it distracting to others?** If one student so severely affects the learning environment for all students, you will need to act.

3. **Is the behavior contagious?** If the behavior (for example, chatting or tapping a desk) has imminent potential to spread to others, you will need to intervene.

4. **Is the student testing the system?** Some students may think it's their responsibility to check whether you are serious about your consequences. If you aren't, don't have those consequences. If they fluctuate based on your energy level (driven by day of the week or time of day, for example), don't have them. Adults need to have clarity on the consequences they are implementing. In the absence of clarity, an adult's response may be inappropriate or poorly timed.

The responses to these questions will determine the immediacy of your actions. As is often the case when it comes to behavior, the more proactively teachers act, the less reactive they need to become. If you believe you have more time to process the situation, Grossman (2004) offers a second set of five questions in total to consider.

1. **Do I have all of the facts?** A disruption between students might require an immediate response to quell the noise, but it's likely beneficial to take advantage of the time to get the facts right. Coming into a disagreement at a later stage increases the potential to view things a certain way. Think of any argument you've ever come across; is it easy to discern who is right? Do you take a side based on your personal views and experiences? Although we may

believe we see the world the way it is, in reality we see the world the way we are, through our lens of personal experience. To ensure they have gained all the facts, teachers should take time, listen to all parties involved in an incident, and be sure not to rely on their previously held views of the students.

2. **Is this the right time?** It is always a mistake to humiliate students in front of their peers. When they are already struggling with emotional balance, this will unfavorably tip the scales. Oftentimes the other students also see this and will view the adult negatively if they think the teacher's response resembles picking on a student who is already experiencing challenges. Intervene privately and quietly. Allowing students to save face isn't a sign of weakness, and it won't undermine your authority. It will give students a clear view of the authentic expectations in the classroom. As an example, if you consider respect a foundational expectation in your classroom, you must demonstrate it even when a student behaves most disrespectfully. You will never teach a student about respect by trying to out-disrespect him or her during his or her difficult moments.

3. **Is the student in the right frame of mind?** If the student is at his or her emotional pinnacle, he or she can become even more disruptive. In these situations, you may need to redirect the student to a quiet place within the classroom (as exists in many primary classrooms) or to a space outside the class (as is more typical in secondary environments). Please use this quiet space judiciously, and don't make it part of a regular routine for certain students.

4. **Am I in the right state of mind?** It's important that educators take time to get emotionally grounded before intervening with students. Students can easily push our buttons, and it becomes even easier if our energy reserves are low. Look at these eight simple words: "I didn't say you had an attitude problem." Now say them eight times in a row, each time switching the emphasis to the succeeding word. Did you notice how the meaning of the statement changed? Now imagine on top of that, you have invaded the student's personal space (proximity) and you are a hand talker. Is it easy to see why the message received might differ from the message intended? If the student perceives a threat of power or control, you might respond more severely than is warranted. What strategies do you have in place for your own checks and balances when dealing with negative behavior? Consider discussing strategies with colleagues. What advice can they offer for dealing with challenging situations? Do you have a colleague who can intervene when you can't reach the right frame of mind or if you need a moment to regroup?

5. **Is this an isolated incident?** Consider whether the student who has acted out seems to be having an off day. In other words, is this an isolated incident for that student? If so, perhaps a quiet word with the student at the end of class might suffice. He or she will likely appreciate that you noticed, and you have the potential there to assist a student experiencing a difficult moment.

Reviewing this section may feel overwhelming, but I would argue that when teachers consider their academic planning and instruction, they work through similar questions that they would apply to academics. If you framed these considerations in academic language, if you were addressing academic skill gaps instead of behavioral skill gaps, would you consider it overwhelming? Good planning for effective behavior takes time; poor planning (or not planning and just reacting) takes even more time. It's often spent in remediating, backtracking, apologizing, and rebuilding. As mentioned previously, Fisher and Frey (2015) note that to raise levels of student achievement, teachers must improve the quality of their relationships with students. It's important to get on the same side as your student, develop collaborative solutions, and teach responsibility.

Once you have determined the action you will take, you will need to ensure you make some effort to follow up. Conversations held with students after you have issued consequences would involve identifying what may have caused the behavior, and could involve establishing strategies for proactively dealing with the behavior before it occurs again. It may take simple questions, like these four, to engage the students in reflection and proactive planning.

1. What happened?
2. What were you thinking or feeling at the time?
3. What impact do you think that behavior had?
4. What might be an alternative behavior you could choose?

Spending time with students to develop replacement behaviors (ones that more closely approximate the desired behaviors than what the students previously exhibited) will have long-term benefits for both the teacher and the students. An example Hierck (2017) mentions involves using a signal card (think traffic light) system. Picture a student whose disruptive behavior is calling out at inappropriate times. This is attention-seeking behavior, and the replacement behavior needs to meet the student's need while also moderating the disruptive behavior. Hierck (2017) explains, "Using a signal card system, [the student] could let the teacher know when [he or] she is green (good to go), yellow (starting to slow), or red (ready to blow) before acting out" (p. 67). The use of an alternative learning environment (a colleague's classroom where he or she can calm down or a walk to the office to say hello to the principal) could also help the student meet his or her need to be noticed. However, the ultimate goal remains the same: helping students close the gaps in their academic and behavioral learning.

The Takeaways

How educators view problem behaviors, and their initial response to those behaviors, plays a significant role in either limiting their impact or fanning the flames to sustain or grow the behaviors. The key ideas from this chapter include the following.

- When a negative behavior occurs in your classroom, changing what you do as an adult is sometimes the best step to take in order to change the behavior.

- Power struggles don't produce positive outcomes; they simply raise the stakes and result in increases in negative behaviors.

- Consequences in isolation do not improve behavior.

- Teaching the desired behaviors is the best approach to altering negative behaviors.

- All behaviors occur for one of two reasons: (1) to get something or (2) to avoid something.

- Grossman (2004) offers a series of reflective questions teachers can pose when deciding on next steps to ameliorate negative behaviors.

- Spending time with students to develop replacement behaviors will have long-term benefits for both the teacher and the students.

- It's important to identify the types of academic and social behaviors that are desirable and then work toward developing them in your classroom.

Before moving on to the epilogue and the case study in the appendix, please reflect on the following questions: What behaviors present the biggest challenge in your classroom and your school? What alternatives to the desired behavior would you and your team be willing to accept as students build their capacity to demonstrate appropriate behaviors?

Epilogue

Throughout the chapters in this book, I have endeavored to provide a rationale for the significance of managing behavior. The concept of behavior management is often viewed with a negative lens, yet my own experience provides many positive memories borne out of working with students to resolve some challenging behaviors and helping them develop more positive replacement behaviors. Many of these positive memories also occurred when the school collectively embraced this approach. As the adage goes, many hands make light work. A few team members cannot have responsibility for the work that faces all members of a school team. Some of the most challenging students in schools will require an all-hands-on-deck mindset in order to alter their behaviors and improve their life chances. In the appendix to their landmark book *Unstoppable Learning*, Fisher and Frey (2015) summarize the managing learning element of the Unstoppable Learning model with table E.1, which provides driving questions, and some excellent talking and thinking points for members of a school community to consider.

Table E.1: Driving Questions for Managing Learning

Students	Teachers	Formal Leaders
• Do I understand the routines and procedures of the classroom? • Will I and my classmates be treated fairly? • Is this a safe place to learn and make errors? • How can I get help when I need it? • When I don't meet my expectations and my teacher's, how can I recover and move forward?	• How do I build and maintain healthy relationships in my classroom? • How do I respond when problematic behaviors occur? • How can I return students with problematic behavior to learning?	• How does the management of the classroom facilitate student learning? • Do students know the ways of work in the classroom? • Does the teacher contribute data to resolve problematic student behaviors?

Source: Adapted from Fisher & Frey, 2015, p. 178.

A significant part of this book has also emphasized the importance of relationships. This does not mean that content is unimportant. In fact, both relationships and content matter, but it's important that teachers establish relationships before addressing academic content. As Fisher and Frey (2015) indicate, "Systems thinking teachers rarely use punitive approaches and see problematic behavior as just one more thing to teach, much like reading, mathematics, fitness, or art appreciation" (p. 13). Building a relationship establishes trust between the teacher and student, allowing each to see the other in a different light. Once a teacher knows a student beyond a score, he or she is more likely to try alternate strategies to ensure learning. Once a student feels he or she is more than a number, the student's effort for that adult changes. Let's also remember that the majority of students will exhibit positive behaviors and engage in learning when they believe their teachers know and care about them. I am certain many readers of this book can provide an example of a student who acted differently in one grade level or class than in another comparable situation simply because of the relationships that had been established. If we build relationships, students will learn.

As you reflect on the chapters and establish your next first steps, please take note of the progress you are making and the impact that has on student outcomes. I am confident that both the progress and the impact will be significant.

As I reflect on the concepts the chapters in this book have addressed, I am drawn to the words of mathematician and educator Seymour Papert (1998), who identified what should still be all educators' desire:

> So the model that says learn while you're at school, while you're young, the skills that you will apply during your lifetime is no longer tenable. The skills that you can learn when you're at school will not be applicable. They will be obsolete by the time you get into the workplace and need them, except for one skill. The one really competitive skill is the skill of being able to learn. It is the skill of being able not to give the right answer to questions about what you were taught in school, but to make the right response to situations that are outside the scope of what you were taught in school. We need to produce people who know how to act when they're faced with situations for which they were not specifically prepared.

As identified throughout this book, the requisite skills for success in life do not reside only in the academic domain. Our students will need to grow their skills in the social behavior and academic behavior domains as well and draw on those skills when they face new and unique challenges in their lives beyond graduation. As educators, we have all made a commitment to improving the life chances of every student we are fortunate to interact with. We know both the academic and behavioral skills students need to function in today's world. Taking a positive, proactive approach to teaching both will ensure that all students are well-positioned for success beyond the walls of the schoolhouse.

APPENDIX

A Case Study: Thomas Jefferson Junior High School

In my consulting work, I appreciate the opportunity to work with a school or district over an extended period of time. That has happened with a school district in Woodridge, Illinois, which has six elementary schools and one junior high school. The focus of this appendix is Thomas Jefferson Junior High School, which has implemented many of the structures and produced many positive outcomes aligned with managing learning.

Offering a model school to colleagues could potentially cause them to misinterpret the school's model as the one and only way to do this work. My notion in highlighting the work of Jefferson is to support school teams in understanding, developing, and implementing the critical components of a positive approach to managing learning. As a former scientist and science teacher, I consider a *model* to be a representation of an idea, process, or system that one can use to describe concepts that readers may not have personal experience with. Models are central to explaining the work successful schools do, both in doing their research and when communicating their results.

This appendix describes how Jefferson set up its system and processes. Perhaps the most significant contributing factor was the relentless focus the school had on mindset and relationship building with and among students, and with and among staff, every day. It also had a clear focus on involving the entire school staff in setting a positive tone as part of the overall initiative every year.

Beginning at the start of the management initiative, and each year thereafter, the following activities occurred during the first week of each school year.

- Personally welcoming students
- Conveying school expectations, with all students rotating through presentations

- Having administration and a guest speaker lead thematic motivational discussions
- Having a week of team-building and problem-solving activities in classrooms

The school then followed up and did the same things to re-establish the tone after winter break and spring break with the same focus.

Another key component of the initiative was the relentless commitment by administration and teachers to hold each other accountable for school-home relationship building. Examples of this included making positive phone calls to start the year (and continuing to make those calls throughout the year) and having a parent phone call or parent-teacher conference anytime student behavior needed to be addressed. These items were non-negotiable, as all members of the school team were committed and held accountable to their implementation.

As you will see in the pages that follow, there is a direct link between academics and social and emotional learning and behavior. Academic growth happened each year over the six-year period from the 2011–2012 to the 2016–2017 school years as the school implemented its new approach toward managing learning (English language arts and mathematics advanced placement scores increased every year, as did Standardized Test for the Assessment of Reading [STAR] and Partnership for Assessment of Readiness for College and Careers [PARCC] scores). Anecdotally, teachers also noted significant student growth in deportment and a reduction in office referrals.

I am indebted to the current and former principals of Jefferson. Principal Justin Warnke provided all the data sets and the analyses in this appendix as well as some thoughts that contributed to the content of this appendix. His predecessor, William Schmidt, reviewed all the content and shared some feedback to ensure alignment with the work he led and the outcomes the school achieved. Justin has greatly assisted in creating the following narrative that highlights the journey of the school as it wrestled with overt behavior challenges and strived to create a positive learning culture for all. Although the school has made significant gains, Justin will be the first to state that the journey is not complete and the collective commitment of the entire school team is to continue to refine and adjust until all the students attain proficiency in the desired outcomes.

Background

Thomas Jefferson Junior High School has approximately 650 students in the seventh and eighth grades and is situated in the village of Woodridge, Illinois, a suburb

Appendix

twenty-five miles west of Chicago. Jefferson has slightly more than 40 percent of students qualifying for free and reduced lunch. The school has a relatively diverse student population, with the demographics for 2016 illustrated in table A.1.

Table A.1: Thomas Jefferson Junior High School Demographic Data for 2016

Student Race or Ethnicity	Percentage
White	44.2
Black	14.3
Hispanic	28.3
Asian	8.3
American Indian or Pacific Islander	0.2
Two or More	4.8

Source: © 2018 by Thomas Jefferson Junior High School. Used with permission.

It's illustrative to go back in time to when much of this work began. In 2011, Jefferson brought in a new administrative team to lead the school. William Schmidt was hired as building principal, Justin Warnke assumed the role of associate principal, and Brianne Malatt served as the dean of students. The building staff were primarily tenured staff whose students had performed relatively well on standardized tests, such as the Illinois Standards Achievement Test, and genuinely cared about students and their growth as individuals.

Despite strong efforts in the classroom, it was evident that student behavior oftentimes presented a distraction to students' learning and teachers' delivery of instruction. Table A.2 (page 84) offers the complete data for office discipline referrals by month for the 2011–2012 school year, including the numbers of days and students involved, and the average monthly office discipline referral rate. The Days Count column reflects the number of days in attendance, the Referral Count column reflects the number of referrals that month, and the Average Office Discipline Referrals per School Day column refers to the average number of referrals written per attendance day.

Of the 1,106 office discipline referrals written that year at Jefferson, 132 referrals resulted in in-school suspensions, and 64 referrals resulted in out-of-school suspensions. See table A.3 (page 84) for the number of days, events, and students involved in these suspensions.

Table A.2: Office Discipline Referral Data for 2011–2012

Month	Days Count	Referral Count	Average Office Discipline Referrals per School Day
August	6	1	0.17
September	21	41	1.95
October	20	140	7.00
November	16	131	8.19
December	12	63	5.25
January	20	117	5.85
February	19	190	10.00
March	16	114	7.13
April	20	165	8.25
May	22	144	6.55
June	3	0	0.00
July	0	0	0.00
Totals:	**175**	**1,106**	**5.03**

Source: © 2018 by Thomas Jefferson Junior High School. Used with permission.

Table A.3: Office Discipline Referrals Leading to Suspension for 2011–2012

	Days	Events	Students Contributing
In-School Suspension	152	132	80
Out-of-School Suspension	165	64	44
Expulsion	0	0	0

Source: © 2018 by Thomas Jefferson Junior High School. Used with permission.

First Year of Behavioral Management Implementation

Over the course of the 2011–2012 school year, Jefferson administration collected baseline discipline data and decided that the school would implement the positive behavioral interventions and supports (PBIS) system to establish consistency, a common language, and common ways to address behavior. PBIS (also referred to in the literature as *schoolwide positive behavior interventions and supports* or *SWPBIS*) is a proactive, systematic, tiered approach to establish the behavioral supports needed in schools to ensure positive learning environments for all students. Buffum, Mattos, Weber, and Hierck (2015) describe the three tiers of the model as follows:

> The base of the pyramid represents primary preventions—schoolwide efforts to teach and positively reinforce the academic and social behaviors needed to succeed in school. As students demonstrate at-risk behavior, support is tiered to provide targeted, supplemental help at the Tier 2 secondary level, and highly individualized, intensive behavior interventions at the Tier 3 tertiary level. (p. 10)

The base of the pyramid represents the first—or universal—tier. Jefferson administration assembled a universal tier PBIS team to spearhead the efforts of developing a schoolwide behavioral system that embraced setting common expectations for student behavior (a schoolwide behavioral matrix), establishing a common approach for addressing student misbehavior, developing a T-chart of office- versus classroom-managed behaviors, and establishing an implementation plan.

The team consisted of nine staff members, covering a wide range of grade levels and content areas, and included both certified and noncertified staff. In addition to developing these primary documents and procedures, the PBIS team also developed a system for rewarding students who demonstrate positive behavior and a system to continuously educate both staff and students on the behavioral expectations both upon implementation and over the course of the year as student behavior escalated. The team built all these documents around the core expectations that staff determined: be respectful, be responsible, and give best effort before, during, and after school. Over the course of the school year, the PBIS team rolled out the documents to Jefferson staff and parents. After meeting with each group, the team revised and adjusted the documents to meet the needs of the students, the building, and the community based on feedback each group provided. Once all documents were finalized, the PBIS team organized documents and electronically shared a folder of the documents with all stakeholders.

The PBIS team then proceeded to develop a plan to roll out the behavioral framework to all staff and students for the next school year and compiled a list of universal tier interventions. In doing so, the team developed the expectation rotation, where students and faculty learned what desired behaviors looked like and how to act in each school (or school-related) environment. This provided all students with a common model for acceptable forms of conduct wherever they would go throughout the building, including the classroom, hallway, restroom, lunchroom, and locker room, and on the bus, before and after school. A secondary benefit to organizing this expectation rotation was that staff would then learn how to appropriately teach or remind students about demonstrating appropriate behavior in each school environment.

Over the course of the school year, the PBIS team provided professional development to staff on the philosophy, structure, and supports offered through the universal tier of the PBIS system that all students would receive. A portion of professional development time was allocated to implementing the PBIS system over the course of the entire 2011–2012 school year.

Based on the work of Tom Hierck, Charlie Coleman, and Chris Weber (2011), the PBIS team also developed a three-step process for addressing minor disruptions in the school. This system included a common expectation that if a student demonstrated a minor disruption in the school, the teacher would redirect him or her. If the student continued to misbehave, the teacher would redirect him or her again. On the third disruptive behavior, the teacher would issue the student a consequence. The consequences that the teacher had at his or her disposal included a parent phone call, a red pass (or a time-out in another teacher's class or a pod area), lunch detention, or after-school detention. This process helped create a common procedure for addressing students who needed reminders about the rules.

The PBIS team selected the School-Wide Information System (SWIS) Suite from PBISApps (see www.pbisapps.org) to track student behavior by focusing on the following data points: student, problem behavior, time, and location. This system would track student misbehavior by tracking office discipline referrals and after-school detentions. The team collected and utilized the data to adjust supervision, provide behavioral support, and create student incentives for demonstrating positive behaviors instead of problematic behaviors.

The team also developed a process for schoolwide intervention for when student misbehavior would arise. The team developed a system for making behavioral improvement lessons (called *cool tools*) that reminded students how to behave in different environments in school. Student behavior data organized and compiled by the SWIS Suite drove these lessons. The behavioral lessons, which the PBIS team recruited Jefferson students to record video of, served to remind students how to behave and not behave in different environments and how to appropriately demonstrate specific behaviors (such as acceptable physical touching and arrival to class on time).

On the flip side, the PBIS team developed a system of positive reinforcement for students who demonstrated positive behavior according to the three schoolwide expectations (be respectful, be responsible, and give best effort). The team created the Jeffy (short for *Jefferson*) as a positive reinforcement ticket. Students could use the tickets they received as raffle tickets to win weekly prizes, such as gym time, computer time, time with staff, or special school privileges (for example, a front seat at an assembly, early access to the lunch line, or a snack bar pass). Students could also use the tickets as currency at the school PBIS store. The PBIS team solicited fellow staff and local businesses that students frequented to compile an inventory of items that students would enjoy. As a result of the PBIS team's efforts, students could purchase many of the following items in the store: school supplies, lotions and soaps, spirit wear, sporting goods, toys, music, videos, games, or privileges. Staff and local businesses donated all store items.

Last, the PBIS team planned schoolwide, grade-level, and team celebrations to recognize behavioral improvements at each level. These celebrations would offer the staff and students the recognition and reinforcement they needed for demonstrating the positive character traits of being respectful and responsible and giving best effort.

Second Year of Behavioral Management Implementation

At the start of the 2012–2013 school year, the school rolled out the universal tier of the PBIS system to students and staff. On the first day of school, staff greeted all students outside and welcomed them into the building. Students and staff began their day with a whole-school assembly, where students and staff learned about the PBIS framework and what all students could expect in the upcoming year. As with all major systemic changes, students and staff needed frequent reminders about the changes in expectations and procedures for handling disruptive behavior. It would have been easy to default to what was comfortable or "the ways things have always been done around here" in these moments. Instead, the staff collectively dug in and committed to the implementation of the new expectations and procedures. They were determined to include celebration and came up with creative ways to celebrate student behavioral success. The staff did a thorough job of organizing field days, whole-school assemblies, and staff-versus-student competitions (for example, adaptations of popular game shows). Also, though the staff had an adjustment period, a majority adopted the new expectations and procedures for addressing student misbehavior, ensuring that they reinforced positive behavior. As a result of strong staff efforts and responsive students, office discipline referral numbers fell drastically. Table A.4 offers data on the number of office discipline referrals by month, comparing the 2011–2012 and 2012–2013 school years, and reflects the decrease in office discipline referrals.

Table A.4: Office Discipline Referrals for 2011–2013

Month	2011–2012	2012–2013
August	1	1
September	41	41
October	140	80

continued →

Month	2011–2012	2012–2013
November	131	62
December	63	39
January	117	72
February	190	61
March	114	43
April	165	108
May	144	78
June	0	0
July	0	0
Totals:	**1,106**	**585**

Source: © 2018 by Thomas Jefferson Junior High School. Used with permission.

In addition to the implementation of the universal tier (tier one) of the PBIS system, Jefferson administration assembled a secondary PBIS team to facilitate the implementation of the secondary tier (tier two) of the PBIS system. This secondary PBIS team consisted of a school social worker, a counselor, an administrator, and four seventh- and eighth-grade teachers from different content areas. The secondary PBIS team's primary mission was to compile a menu of behavioral supports for students who did not respond to the common behavioral expectations, or tier one supports. The menu the secondary PBIS team developed contained a list of behavioral interventions that staff could easily administer and had set entrance criteria, exit criteria, and monitoring procedures. The list of interventions that the secondary PBIS team developed included CICO, check and connect (a proactive support strategy meant as a preventative action, involving regular check-ins with high-risk students bordering on needing tier three intervention), self-monitoring, behavioral incentives, behavior contracts, small-group counseling, and tier two behavioral intervention classes (these classes provided behavioral support around decision making, organization, goal setting, and emotional management).

After developing the menu of support, the secondary PBIS team established specific criteria for entering the interventions (these included any of the following: three office discipline referrals in one month, four minor disciplinary consequences in two weeks, four visits to the student services team in two weeks, or a 10 percent or higher absentee rate) and developed procedures for professional development for the staff around this tier of support. After much discussion, the secondary PBIS team agreed that the majority of professional development would go into training staff how to execute the CICO behavioral intervention (described in chapter 4, page 57), as staff would use that intervention when working with struggling students. Specifically, staff received training on how to conference with students when it was time to check in, conference when students were checking out, accurately award points around a behavioral goal, and discretely complete a daily progress report card. The secondary PBIS team took the staff through a variety of simulations on how to perform each step of the intervention, and nearly all staff signed up to become prospective CICO mentors. Any staff members involved in CICO need to have a desire to build a relationship with the student. This intervention will not work if the adult believes his or her role is simply to record negative behaviors as a means to escalating consequences. The power of the CICO intervention lies in three main areas.

1. Setting a shared behavioral goal for the student directly aligned to the behavioral matrix
2. Providing the student with feedback related to his or her behavioral goal
3. Helping track student behavioral progress over time

Essentially, in this intervention, students report to an assigned mentor teacher of their choice for a brief check-in to make sure they are set with their materials and to get a short pep talk in the morning. The students traditionally carry a daily progress report card and receive feedback from their teachers on their performance around the shared goal. Students carry their daily progress report card around for the week, gathering feedback (points) from teachers to measure their success with behavior over time while participating in the intervention. The students then check out with their mentor teacher, where they celebrate good times over the course of the day and discuss areas for improvement that may have arisen. The goal is ultimately to show the students that they can behave appropriately on their own without a teacher telling them to or without carrying a piece of paper.

Third Year of Behavioral Management Implementation

During the 2013–2014 school year, Jefferson staff implemented the secondary tier of the PBIS system while continuing to improve the universal tier. The importance of this secondary tier was to provide students who needed a little more support or feedback with the help they needed to have success within the regular classroom. In the first year of tier two implementation, many students benefited from the interventions, especially CICO. However, a couple of situations arose that made CICO ineffective for some students. The first hurdle was that certain students refused to carry the daily progress report card. Some found it stigmatizing and embarrassing. Another problem that occurred with the daily progress report cards was that certain students would lose (or intentionally throw away) their cards if they did not meet their points goal or get the score they wanted. Students would occasionally not give cards to teachers because they knew their behavior was not perfect. Over the course of the year, for the students who were often guilty of throwing daily progress report cards away or not responsible about giving them to staff members, the teachers completed daily progress report cards electronically. This way, students did not need to carry the cards, look different from other students, or remember to provide them to the teachers for feedback.

A challenge emerged over the course of the school year when the faculty struggled to identify all students who qualified for the intervention as a result of poor documentation and parent contact. A key component of the three-step CICO process is documenting disciplinary consequences and parent contact in the student information system. Many parents of students needing intervention did not receive phone calls. This required resetting expectations for staff on calling home for behavioral concerns. After resetting the expectations, the PBIS team was able to identify more students for the CICO program. Once students in need received additional intervention or combinations of tier two interventions, the school saw an additional drop in office discipline referrals. This could mainly be attributed to a stronger interpretation of the PBIS universal tier and students' receiving the behavioral support needed. See table A.5 for data on this reduction in referrals per month.

Table A.5: Office Discipline Referrals for 2011–2014

Month	2011–2012	2012–2013	2013–2014
January	117	72	35
February	190	61	58
March	114	43	90
April	165	108	56
May	144	78	49
June	0	0	10
July	0	0	0
August	1	1	4
September	41	41	9
October	140	80	50
November	131	62	41
December	63	39	37
Totals:	**1,106**	**585**	**439**

Source: © 2018 by Thomas Jefferson Junior High School. Used with permission.

Appendix

To complete the behavioral support, Jefferson administration assembled a tertiary PBIS team to plan for the implementation of the third tier of the PBIS system. This team comprised the school psychologist, a school administrator, a counselor, a school social worker, and a teacher representative. The tertiary PBIS team developed a menu of support that specifically serviced students who did not respond to tier one or tier two of the PBIS system, or who were in emotional distress (for example, potentially suicidal). This third tier recognizes that behavior could escalate quickly and services need to be designed to appropriately respond and completely support the child and family. The services offered at this tier included the following: functional behavioral analysis (a method of determining why a student acts a certain way, including looking at nonacademic factors that might be contributing to some frustration with learning), a behavioral intervention plan, and wraparound services (individual counseling for the student at school or in the community, and counseling or related supports for the family). A student receiving wraparound services might qualify for one service, a combination of services, or all three. After the tertiary PBIS team developed supports and created a concise system for delivery of services, team members communicated to staff what tier three supports were and explained how students qualified for them and how this third tier was highly responsive and data driven.

Fourth Year of Behavioral Management Implementation

In 2014–2015, Jefferson officially implemented its third and final phase of the PBIS system. As the research (Hierck et al., 2011) suggests, approximately 1–5 percent of students qualify for this level of support at any given time over the course of the school year. At the same time, the faculty also implemented Kagan Cooperative Learning strategies (Kagan, 1994). Social skills are a major component of the Kagan strategies, and these team-building and class-building strategies helped to promote a safe and caring environment for all learners. These strategies are rich in teaching and reinforcing social skills, and they foster team-building and class-building structures in order to develop a learning environment that is conducive to working in teams of students. The PIES principles (positive interdependence, individual accountability, equal participation, and simultaneous interaction; Kagan, n.d.) support these strategies and ensure that all students work together to find success within the cooperative structure (see chapter 3, page 31). Every student has responsibility for performing in front of his or her peers, every student has equal time to share, and the bulk of students participate at the same time. When these components are in place, students feel that they are on the same team and have equal status. They feel compelled to participate and intellectually and socially engaged in a proactive fashion.

Jefferson utilized class-building and team-building structures to enhance the work of Significant 72 (see chapter 2, page 25) at the beginning of the year and reinforce this initiative daily throughout the school year. By setting the expectation that *all* teachers implement Kagan Cooperative Learning structures for the purposes of both instruction and class building or team building, staff were able to develop a safe learning environment that helped promote students in getting acquainted, forming team identity, providing mutual support, valuing differences, and developing synergy. As students develop these components, they feel safe and willing to share within their team and throughout the class in creating a positive culture for learning.

Through an extremely intensive layer of tertiary PBIS, staff implemented supports and afforded significant attention to the universal tier (tier one) for social skills and classroom culture development through team building and class building. A significant increase in hospitalizations for suicidal ideation and depression among students reflected the success of these efforts in identifying students who needed support. To help continue to identify students who were in emotional pain, Jefferson began surveying staff utilizing the DESSA (Devereux Student Strengths Assessment; www.apertureed.com/dessa-overview) and a homegrown survey that determined at what level the student was connected to Jefferson and if he or she felt that he or she had a strong connection to at least one staff member. From this, Jefferson developed the wall of students, an activity that staff engaged in to show that every student deserved a positive connection with an adult in the school. Teachers printed a copy of every student's ID card and put them on the wall in a secluded hallway that only teachers could access. Teachers then removed the cards of any student they built a connection with. They would then discuss any students who were left on the wall, to ensure every student had an adult champion. This activity provided staff with a visual as to whether a student identified an adult he or she felt he or she had a relationship with, and as to which students the staff had a relationship with. It also helped specifically identify the students who were falling through the cracks. This activity helped the student services team provide intervention and connect the students to the school, and helped facilitate the relationship development between students and teachers.

After Jefferson employed the universal and tertiary interventions, the school collected student referral data. Table A.6 reflects referral days per month.

During the 2014–2015 school year, the seventh-grade cohort provided significant emotional challenges, which indicated that the school would need to systemically alter supervision and frequency of tier one, two, and three interventions. After working with the challenging seventh-grade cohort, school administrators determined that for the next school year, they needed to provide all students and staff with training and reminders around perseverance and growth mindset development. To do this, staff needed instruction about critical differences between people who have fixed

Appendix

Table A.6: Office Discipline Referrals for 2011–2015

Month	2011–2012	2012–2013	2013–2014	2014–2015
January	117	72	35	71
February	190	61	58	39
March	114	43	90	71
April	165	108	56	76
May	144	78	49	58
June	0	0	10	19
July	0	0	0	0
August	1	1	4	0
September	41	41	9	45
October	140	80	50	47
November	131	62	41	39
December	63	39	37	64
Totals:	**1,106**	**585**	**439**	**529**

Source: © 2018 by Thomas Jefferson Junior High School. Used with permission.

mindsets and people who have growth mindsets. The school leaders simply clarified this concept for staff and students by offering this information based on the work of Dweck (2006): people with a growth mindset believe talent and intelligence can grow through hard work and attitude. Talent is not predetermined. Alternatively, people with a fixed mindset worry not about challenging themselves and getting better but about saving face and constantly proving themselves right. In a fixed mindset, failing or getting things wrong is devastating—not a learning opportunity.

Staff members were provided with resources about growth mindset. They devoted fifteen minutes per day to developing a growth mindset in students and staff, or completing commercial surveys around a growth mindset, grit, and perseverance, to monitor student attitude. The staff received professional development on how to help promote positive self-talk with students and on how to reframe self-deprecating messages that students say when facing failure (for example, "I made a mistake" changes to "Mistakes help me improve," or "This is too hard" changes to "This is going to take some time and effort"). Despite the constant reminders and quarterly events to excite students and promote perseverance, grit, and a growth mindset, unfortunately, there was an overall increase in student misbehavior despite improving in the first couple of months. The data sets in table A.7 (page 94) reflect the challenges the Jefferson staff faced.

Table A.7: Office Discipline Referrals for 2011–2016

Month	2011–2012	2012–2013	2013–2014	2014–2015	2015–2016
January	117	72	35	71	68
February	190	61	58	39	89
March	114	43	90	71	88
April	165	108	56	76	70
May	144	78	49	58	124
June	0	0	10	19	11
July	0	0	0	0	0
August	1	1	4	0	0
September	41	41	9	45	37
October	140	80	50	47	53
November	131	62	41	39	66
December	63	39	37	64	49
Totals:	**1,106**	**585**	**439**	**529**	**655**

Source: © 2018 by Thomas Jefferson Junior High School. Used with permission.

Sixth Year of Behavioral Management Implementation

During the fifth year of implementation, the 2015–2016 school year, the staff received training to provide more engaging instruction and worked with students on perseverance, continuing the PBIS work. Data trends continued throughout this year, and the school made no significant changes to the implementation of their initiative. For this reason, we'll jump ahead to examining the sixth year of implementation. In the 2016–2017 school year, staff decided they needed to improve the way they taught student behavior, and they needed to regularly reteach student behavioral expectations and boost incentives for demonstrating positive behaviors. Essentially, they needed to go back to the basics of the universal tier of PBIS and inject some new energy into it. This is a reminder that quality work is not about arriving; it's about continually striving. The reality of our profession is that the work is never really completed and it does not align with a checklist. Although it's important to bring in new structures to achieve the desired results, true success always resides in the culture of your school. Every year in a school is different. Every group of students is unique, as is every faculty. So over the course of the school year, the staff continued to inspire students with quarterly assemblies to promote a growth mindset and perseverance, and through weekly activities to reinforce these skills. In addition to the further development of these mindset activities, the school also revamped its high-risk student screener, moving from the DESSA to the Review360 behavior management system, explicitly utilizing the Behavioral and Emotional Screening System (BESS) and Panorama's social-emotional learning screeners to identify students who needed behavioral support or counseling for mental health concerns. These screeners helped identify and support students who struggled with managing their emotions and regulating their behavior at school. After a lot of reflection and continuous improvement, Jefferson was able to again reduce overall student misbehavior for the 2016–2017 school year—this time to an all-time low (see table A.8).

Table A.8: Office Discipline Referrals for 2011–2017

Month	2011–2012	2012–2013	2013–2014	2014–2015	2015–2016	2016–2017
January	1	72	35	71	68	27
February	41	61	58	39	89	34
March	140	43	90	71	88	47
April	131	108	56	76	70	55
May	63	78	49	58	124	82
June	117	0	10	19	11	7
July	190	0	0	0	0	0
August	114	1	4	0	0	0
September	165	41	9	45	37	24
October	144	80	50	47	53	28
November	0	62	41	39	66	24
December	0	39	37	64	49	16
Totals:	1,106	585	439	529	655	344

Source: © 2018 by Thomas Jefferson Junior High School. Used with permission.

The Work Ahead

After collecting data for six years while using quality strategies like PBIS, Kagan Cooperative Learning, and growth mindset development, and improving student screening tools and protocols, the leadership determined that it needed to continue to enhance the tier one support offered to students and staff. To ensure this support, Jefferson instituted Kagan, Kyle, and Scott's (2004) Win-Win Discipline program. The premise of this program is to focus on appropriately identifying the type of disruption and a student's position (function of the behavior) and meeting the student's behavioral need. The program suggests that student disruptions are irresponsible or immature attempts at meeting behavioral needs.

In the 2017–2018 school year, Jefferson fully implemented the Win-Win Discipline program in order to truly understand why students misbehave. The training and ongoing professional development helped staff establish preventative procedures to meet students' needs in the classroom, develop an effective toolbox of structures to manage student misbehavior in the moment of disruption, and develop structures to follow up with students after a disruption in the classroom. The ultimate goals of Win-Win Discipline are to ensure that the student and teacher are on the same side, the teacher and student develop collaborative solutions to disruptions, and the teacher ultimately teaches the student learned responsibility. To help implement this, the leadership team started a Win-Win Discipline book club as a structured opportunity for staff members to digest the work of Kagan, Kyle, and Scott (2004). This book club has given staff a safe place to develop fluency, put structures in place to respond to disruptions in the moment, and practice follow-up supports in a safe environment before trying to implement aspects of the program with students. This has also allowed staff to build fluency and proficiency with the structures.

Moving forward, the leadership team has made a collective commitment to continue to reduce behavioral incidents and improve the culture for learning in all classrooms. In the long term, the team hopes that students will know that the staff validate their feelings and that they have a safe environment in which to learn and work as part of the larger school community. It is the goal of the Jefferson staff to meet the social-emotional needs of students while providing a rigorous curriculum. The work has had a positive impact through addressing behavioral concerns and creating a safe learning environment for students. The work has also had a very evident impact on learning outcomes in the academic domain, as increases in academic performance have accompanied the drop in negative behaviors (measured by the office discipline referrals). The hallmark of the educators at this school has become their strong desire to analyze the evidence and make the necessary adjustments to achieve the kinds of results they insist are possible for all students. They don't insist on getting the work right the first time, or all the time. They aim to respond to the evidence, make adjustments to practice, and monitor the impact of those adjustments. The model that Jefferson has put in place is possible at any school site.

The Takeaways

This appendix provided a model for colleagues to consider as they plan the work of implementing a positive approach to managing learning. The key ideas from this appendix include the following.

- Tracking data and monitoring the impact of initiatives are critical.
- Celebration and recognition are key components of a successful journey to school improvement.
- Leadership matters—from both the formal roles and the informal roles of teacher leaders.

Now that you have examined this case study of how Thomas Jefferson Junior High School conducted a pilot program for approaching classroom management, please reflect on the following questions: What pilot program are you and your team prepared to try in service of *all* students' positive behavior? Is there an aspect of this case study that would make an appropriate starting point or next step?

References and Resources

Acredolo, L., & Goodwyn, S. (2005). *Baby hearts: A guide to giving your child an emotional head start*. New York: Bantam Books.

Bascia, N., & Hargreaves, A. (2000). *The sharp edge of educational change: Teaching, leading, and the realities of reform*. London: Routledge.

Biggs, J. B., & Collis, K. F. (1982). *Evaluating the quality of learning: The SOLO taxonomy (structure of the observed learning outcome)*. New York: Academic Press.

Billson, J. M. (1986). The college classroom as a small group: Some implications for teaching and learning. *Teaching Sociology, 14*(3), 143–151.

Buffum, A., Mattos, M., & Weber, C. (2009). *Pyramid response to intervention: RTI, professional learning communities, and how to respond when kids don't learn*. Bloomington, IN: Solution Tree Press.

Buffum, A., Mattos, M., & Weber, C. (2010). The why behind RTI. *Educational Leadership, 68*(2), 10–16.

Buffum, A., Mattos, M., Weber, C., & Hierck, T. (2015). *Uniting academic and behavior interventions: Solving the skill or will dilemma*. Bloomington, IN: Solution Tree Press.

Carnegie Mellon University. (n.d.). *What are the benefits of group work?* Accessed at www.cmu.edu/teaching/designteach/design/instructionalstrategies/groupprojects/benefits.html on May 11, 2018.

Cassetta, G., & Sawyer, B. (2013). *No more taking away recess and other problematic discipline practices*. Portsmouth, NH: Heinemann.

Chang, H. N., & Romero, M. (2008). *Present, engaged, and accounted for: The critical importance of addressing chronic absence in the early grades*. New York: National Center for Children in Poverty.

Cooper, J. O., Heron, T. E., & Heward, W. L. (2007). *Applied behavior analysis* (2nd ed.). Upper Saddle River, NJ: Pearson Education.

Dickens, C. (1843). *A Christmas Carol*. London: Chapman and Hall.

Donohoo, J. (2017). *Collective efficacy: How educators' beliefs impact student learning*. Thousand Oaks, CA: Corwin Press.

DuFour R. (2011). Work together: But only if you want to. *Phi Delta Kappan, 92*(5), 57–61.

DuFour, R., DuFour, R., Eaker, R., Many, T. W., & Mattos, M. (2016). *Learning by doing: A handbook for Professional Learning Communities at Work®* (3rd ed.). Bloomington, IN: Solution Tree Press.

Dweck, C. S. (2006). *Mindset: The new psychology of success.* New York: Ballantine Books.

Eaker, R., & Keating, J. (2008). A shift in school culture: Collective commitments focus on change that benefits student learning. *Journal of Staff Development, 39*(3), 14–17.

Eldred-Cohen, C. (2017). *How Satoshi Tajiri's autism helped create Pokemon.* Acessed at https://the-art-of-autism.com/how-satoshi-tajiris-autism-helped-create-pokemon on July 23, 2018.

Erkens, C. (2016). *Collaborative common assessments: Teamwork. Instruction. Results.* Bloomington, IN: Solution Tree Press.

Erkens, C., Schimmer, T., & Vagle, N. D. (2018). *Instructional agility: Responding to assessment with real-time decisions.* Bloomington, IN: Solution Tree Press.

Fiarman, S. E. (2016). Unconscious bias: When good intentions aren't enough. *Educational Leadership, 74*(3), 10–15.

Fisher, D., & Frey, N. (2015). *Unstoppable learning: Seven essential elements to unleash student potential.* Bloomington, IN: Solution Tree Press.

Fredrickson, B. L. (2013). Positive emotions broaden and build. In P. Devine & A. Plant (Eds.), *Advances in experimental social psychology* (Vol. 47, pp. 1–53). Burlington, MA: Academic Press.

Freiberg, H. J. (2013). Classroom management and student achievement. In J. Hattie & E. M. Anderman (Eds.), *International guide to student achievement* (pp. 228–230). New York: Routledge.

Fullan, M. (2007). *Leading in a culture of change* (Rev. ed.). San Francisco, CA: Jossey-Bass.

Galbraith, J. K. (2001). *The essential Galbraith* (A. D. Williams, Ed.). New York: Mariner Books.

Ginott, H. G. (1972). *Teacher and child: A book for parents and teachers.* New York: Macmillan.

Grossman, H. (2004). *Classroom behavior management for diverse and inclusive schools* (3rd ed.). Lanham, MD: Rowman & Littlefield.

Hattie, J. (2009). *Visible learning: A synthesis of over 800 meta-analyses relating to achievement.* New York: Routledge.

Hattie, J. (2012). *Visible learning for teachers: Maximizing impact on learning.* New York: Routledge.

Hattie, J., & Timperley, H. (2007). The power of feedback. *Review of Educational Research, 77*(1), 81–112.

Hierck, T. (2017). *Seven keys to a positive learning environment in your classroom.* Bloomington, IN: Solution Tree Press.

Hierck, T., Coleman, C., & Weber, C. (2011). *Pyramid of behavior interventions: Seven keys to a positive learning environment.* Bloomington, IN: Solution Tree Press.

Hierck, T., & Freese, A. (2018). *Assessing unstoppable learning.* Bloomington, IN: Solution Tree Press.

Hierck, T., & Peterson, K. (2017). *The positive school culture inventory (PSCI): Purpose, rationale, and development* [White paper]. Accessed at https://cms.azed.gov/home/GetDocumentFile?id=5a8c9d213217e10904f24ea0 on March 14, 2018.

References and Resources

Hierck, T., & Weber, C. (2014). *RTI is a verb*. Thousand Oaks, CA: Corwin Press.

Hoy, A. W., & Weinstein, C. S. (2006). Student and teacher perspectives on classroom management. In C. M. Evertson & C. S. Weinstein (Eds.), *Handbook of classroom management: Research, practice, and contemporary issues* (pp. 181–219). Mahwah, NJ: Erlbaum.

Kagan, S. (n.d.). *Structures optimize engagement*. Accessed at www.kaganonline.com/free_articles/dr_spencer_kagan/ASK28.php on April 30, 2018.

Kagan, S. (1994). *Cooperative learning*. San Clemente, CA: Kagan.

Kagan, S., Kyle, P., & Scott, S. (2004). *Win-Win Discipline: Strategies for all discipline problems*. San Clemente, CA: Kagan.

Kwong, D., & Davis, J. R. (2015). School climate for academic success: A multilevel analysis of school climate and student outcomes. *Journal of Research in Education, 25*(2), 68–81.

Lesnick, J., Goerge, R. M., Smithgall, C., & Gwynne, J. (2010). *Reading on grade level in third grade: How is it related to high school performance and college enrollment? A longitudinal analysis of third-grade students in Chicago in 1996–97 and their educational outcomes* (A report to the Annie E. Casey Foundation). Accessed at www.aecf.org/m/resourcedoc/aecf-ReadingonGradeLevelLongAnal-2010.PDF on March 14, 2018.

Lewis, T. J., Scott, T. M., & Sugai, G. (1994). The problem behavior questionnaire: A teacher-based instrument to develop functional hypotheses of problem behavior in general education classrooms. *Assessment for Effective Intervention, 19*(2–3), 103–115.

Lippman, L., & Schmitz, H. (2013). *What can schools do to build resilience in their students?* Accessed at www.childtrends.org/what-can-schools-do-to-build-resilience-in-their-students on August 5, 2018.

Livingstone, R. W. (1941). *The future in education*. Cambridge, England: Cambridge University Press.

Losen, D. J., Keith, M. A., II, Hodson, C. L., Martinez, T. E., & Belway, S. (2015). *Closing the school discipline gap in California: Signs of progress*. Los Angeles: The Center for Civil Rights Remedies.

Losen, D. J., Martinez, T. E., & Okelola, V. (2014). *Keeping California's kids in school: Fewer students of color missing school for minor misbehavior*. Los Angeles: The Center for Civil Rights Remedies. Accessed at www.civilrightsproject.ucla.edu/resources/projects/center-for-civil-rights-remedies/school-to-prison-folder/summary-reports/keeping-californias-kids-in-school/WithChange.pdf on March 14, 2018.

Madden, W. (2014). *Management 101: Set clear expectations*. Accessed at www.steamfeed.com/management-101-set-clear-expectations on October 16, 2014.

Medbery, J., & Hierck, T. (2017). *The 4 attributes that ensure successful culture and climate initiatives* [White paper]. Accessed at http://go.kickboardforschools.com/LP_Q217-07_MKT_4-attributes-successful-culture on March 14, 2018.

Meichenbaum, D. (n.d.). *How educators can nurture resilience in high-risk children and their families*. Accessed at www.teachsafeschools.org/Resilience.pdf on August 6, 2018.

Muhammad, A. (2018). *Transforming school culture: How to overcome staff division* (2nd ed.). Bloomington, IN: Solution Tree Press.

Murphy, S., & Faulkner, D. (2000). Learning to collaborate: Can young children develop better communication strategies through collaboration with a more popular peer. *European Journal of Psychology of Education, 15*(4), 389–404.

National School Climate Center. (2010). *National school climate standards: Benchmarks to promote effective teaching, learning and comprehensive school improvement.* New York: Author. Accessed at www.schoolclimate.org/themes/schoolclimate/assets/pdf/policy/school-climate-standards.pdf on July 23, 2018.

National Scientific Council on the Developing Child. (2015). *Supportive relationships and active skill-building strengthen the foundations of resilience: Working paper 13.* Accessed at https://46y5eh11fhgw3ve3ytpwxt9r-wpengine.netdna-ssl.com/wp-content/uploads/2015/05/The-Science-of-Resilience2.pdf on July 23, 2018.

National Survey of Student Engagement. (2006). *Engaged learning: Fostering success for all students* (Annual report 2006). Bloomington: Indiana University Center for Postsecondary Research.

National Survey of Student Engagement. (2016). *Engagement insights: Survey findings on the quality of undergraduate education.* Bloomington: Indiana University Center for Postsecondary Research.

Nottingham, J. (n.d.). *Learning pit.* Accessed at https://jamesnottingham.co.uk/learning-pit on May 3, 2018.

Organisation for Economic Co-operation and Development. (2017). *PISA 2015 results: Collaborative problem solving* (Vol. 5). Paris: Author.

Oxford University Press. (2008). *Oxford American large print dictionary.* New York: Author.

Papert, S. (1998, June 2). *Child power: Keys to the new learning of the digital century.* Paper presented at the 11th Colin Cherry Memorial Lecture on Communication, London, England. Accessed at www.papert.org/articles/Childpower.html on May 9, 2018.

Quy, P. H. P. (2017). Group dynamics: Building a sense of belonging in the EFL classroom. *English Teaching Forum, 55*(1), 14–21.

Schlechty, P. C. (1997). *Inventing better schools: An action plan for educational reform.* San Francisco: Jossey-Bass.

Shortage of farmers creates 'dangerous situation' for U.S. (2014, April 15). Accessed at www.nbcnews.com/business/economy/shortage-farmers-creates-dangerous-situation-u-s-n78251 on May 30, 2018.

Sinek, S. (2009). *Start with why: How great leaders inspire everyone to take action.* New York: Portfolio.

Smith, D., Fisher, D., & Frey, N. (2015). *Better than carrots or sticks: Restorative practices for positive classroom management.* Alexandria, VA: Association for Supervision and Curriculum Development.

Speck, M. (1996). *A handbook for implementing year-round education in the high school.* San Diego, CA: National Association for Year-Round Education.

Varga, M. (2017). The effect of teacher-student relationships on the academic engagement of students (Unpublished master's thesis). Goucher College Master of Education. Accessed at https://mdsoar.org/bitstream/handle/11603/3893/VargaMeagan_paper.pdf?sequence=1&isAllowed=y on July 26, 2018.

Walker, B., & Soule, S. A. (2017). Changing company culture requires a movement, not a mandate. *Harvard Business Review*. Accessed at https://hbr.org/2017/06/changing-company-culture-requires-a-movement-not-a-mandate on May 25, 2018.

Weber, C. (2018). *Behavior: The forgotten curriculum*. Bloomington, IN: Solution Tree Press.

Wiggins, A. (2017). *The best class you never taught: How spider web discussion can turn students into learning leaders*. Alexandria, VA: Association for Supervision and Curriculum Development.

Williams, K. C., & Hierck, T. (2015). *Starting a movement: Building culture from the inside out in professional learning communities*. Bloomington, IN: Solution Tree Press.

Index

5-4-3-2-1 strategy, 40

A
ABC tool, 51, 54–55, 62
academic achievement, 45
academic behaviors, 67–68, 78
   defined, 67
   prioritizing, 68
adapting learning, 3
addressing student needs, 70–72
aligning classroom culture, 16–18
assessing learning, 3

B
Bascia, N., 17
behavior management. *See* managing behaviors
Behavioral and Emotional Screening System, 95
Belway, S., 69
Biggs, J. B., 49
Billson, J., 39
Buffum, A., 35, 85
bullying, 38

C
Carnegie Mellon University, 34
Cassetta, G., 48, 68–70
Challenging Learning, 49, 52–54
Chang, H. N., 1
Check-In Check-Out (CICO) strategy, 57–58, 63, 88–90
Christmas Carol, A (Dickens), 4
CICO. *See* Check-In Check-Out strategy
class building, 38–40
class meetings, 58
Coleman, C., 86

collaborative skills. *See* group work; peer relationships
collective commitment, 12, 36, 68–69, 96–97
   to cultural change, 15–16
Collis, K. F., 49–50
communication, 4, 32
   conflict resolution skills, 33
consistency, 3
consolidating learning, 3
Cooper, J., 56
cooperative learning, 40–42

D
daily tasks and routines, 58
Davis, J. R., 45
defiance, 69–70
   addressing student needs, 70–72
   pairing consequences with instruction, 72–73
   responses to, 70
   teaching resilience, 74–75
Devereux Student Strengths Assessment (DESSA), 92, 95
Dickens, C., 4
direct to correct to connect strategy, 60
DNA activities, 55, 57
Donohoo, J., 15
dropout rates, 45
DuFour, R., 14–15
Dweck, C. S., 12, 50, 93
dynamism, 26, 29

E
Eaker, R., 15, 17
effect size, 25, 39
effective feedback, 32
Einstein, A., 4

Eldred-Cohen, C., 29
emotional control, 68
empathy, 38
engagement, 68
equal participation, 41–43
Erkens, C., 31, 34, 39
executive function skills, 67–68
expectations, 35–36
    managing timing of, 24–25
    modeling, 29, 36, 58, 81
    setting, 22–24

F

Faulkner, D., 38
Fiarman, S. E., 36, 43
Fisher, D., 2–4, 7, 9–10, 21, 23–25, 27–29, 32, 35, 37–38, 45, 49, 67, 70–71, 73, 77, 79–80
four H greetings, 28
four-step inquiry process, 49–50
Fredrickson, B. L., 59
Freese, A., 4
Freiberg, H. J., 24
Frey, N., 2–4, 7, 9–10, 21, 23–25, 27–29, 32, 35, 37–38, 45, 49, 67, 70–71, 73, 77, 79–80
Fullan, M., 17
Fundamentalists, 14–16

G

Galbraith, J. K., 14
Ginott, H. G., 27–28
Goerge, R. M., 2
Grossman, H., 75, 78
group work, 31–32, 42–43, 48–49
    behavior and, 35–36
    benefits of, 32–34
    cautions about, 34–35
    cooperative learning, 40–42
    team building, 39–40, 82
groupthink, 34
growth mindset, 33
Gwynne, J., 2

H

Hargreaves, A., 17
Hattie, J., 10, 25–29, 39
Hawthorne effect, 69
Heron, T., 66

Heward, W., 66
Hierck, T., 4, 13, 16–17, 21, 25, 27, 31, 35, 38, 46–48, 51, 54, 59, 62, 68, 71–74, 77, 85–86, 91
Hodson, C. L., 69
Hoy, A. W., 73

I

immediacy, 26–27, 29
inappropriate language, 70–71
individual accountability, 41–43
ineffective practices, 9–11, 18, 35
intentional positivity, 46–47, 61
    outcomes, 47–48
intervention
    when and if, 75–78
Investment Friend project, 27

J

Johnson, D., 27
journaling, 74

K

Kagan Cooperative Learning, 38, 91–92, 95
Kagan, S., 40–43, 70, 91–92, 95–96
Keating, J., 17
Keith, M. A., 69
Kwong, D., 45
Kyle, P., 70, 95–96

L

leading learning, 3
Learning Challenge, 49–50, 52–53
learning gaps, 1–2
learning pit, 49–50, 52–54, 61
Lesnick, J., 2
Lewis, T. J., 55–56
Lippman, L., 74
Livingstone, R. W., 49
Losen, D. J., 69

M

Madden, W., 23
Malatt, B., 83
managing behaviors, 1–2
    ABC tool, 51, 54–55, 62
    behavior support strategies, 55
    case study, 81–97

Index

Check-In Check-Out (CICO) strategy, 57–58, 63, 88–90
class meetings, 58
collective approach to, 1–19
daily tasks and routines, 58
direct to correct to connect strategy, 60
DNA activities, 55, 57
group dynamics, 35–36
group work and peer relationships, 31–42
positive environment, 45–51
practice, review, and model expectations, 58
Problem Behavior Questionnaire, 55–56
responding to problems, 65–75
setting expectations, 22–24
STORY strategy, 59
strategies and tools, 51, 60–61
systems thinking, 2–5
three-to-one praise ratio, 59–60
two-by-ten strategy, 58
Yet strategy, 60
See also problem behaviors
managing learning, 3, 10–11
case study, 81–97
communication and, 6
driving questions, 79
relationships and, 6
responsiveness and, 6
sustainability and, 6
systems thinking, 5–6
Many, T. W., 15
Martinez, T. E., 69
Mattos, M., 15, 35, 85
Medbery, J., 16–17, 31
Meichenbaum, D., 74
metacognitive practices, 68
micromanagement, 23
mission drift, 35–36
motivation to learn, 45
Muhammad, A., 11–12, 14, 17
Murphy, S., 38

N

National School Climate Center, 45
National Scientific Council on the Developing Child, 32
National Survey of Student Engagement, 32–33
negative behaviors. *See* problem behaviors
Nottingham, J., 49–50

O

online resources, 38–39, 54, 57, 86, 92
opting out, 34
Organisation for Economic Co-operation and Development, 68
Oxford University Press, 34

P

pairing consequences with instruction, 70, 72–73
Panorama, 95
Papert, S., 80
peer relationships, 31–32, 42–43, 48–49
cooperative learning, 40–42
Significant 72 project, 38
sociogram of, 37–38
support strategies, 36–37
team building, 39–40, 82
Peterson, K., 47–48
PIES principles, 40–42, 91
Pinterest, 39
planning learning, 3
positive behavioral interventions and supports (PBIS) system, 84–95
positive interdependence, 40–43
positive learning environments, 11, 51–55, 60–61
behavior support, 55–60
best practice, 48–49, 61
building, 45–47
essential beliefs for, 17–18
learning pit, 49–50, 52–54, 61
outcomes, 47–48
practices that promote, 19
Problem Behavior Questionnaire, 55–56
teacher-student relationships, 21–29
power struggles, 10–11, 78
Problem Behavior Questionnaire, 55–56
problem behaviors, 1–2, 6–7, 65–66, 78
academic behaviors, 67–68
defiance, 69–75
educator's responsibility, 66–67
interventions, 75–78
motivators of, 66, 78
social behaviors, 67–69

Q

Quy, P. H. P., 34

R

relationships, 4, 15–16
    alignment to managing learning, 5
    peer, 31–43, 72, 82
    teacher-student, 21–29, 36, 80
relaxation techniques, 74
resilience, 74–75
responsiveness, 4
    alignment to managing learning, 6
Review360 behavior management system, 95
Romero, M., 1

S

Sawyer, B., 48, 68–70
Schimmer, T., 31, 34, 39
Schlechty, P. C., 11
Schleicher, A., 68
Schmidt, W., 82, 83
Schmitz, H., 74
school climate. *See* positive learning environments
school culture, 11–12, 18
    aligning, 16–18
    assessing current, 16
    collective commitment to change, 13–16
school satisfaction, 45
school structure, 11–12
school violence, 45
School-Wide Information System (SWIS) Suite, 86
schoolwide positive behavior interventions and supports (SWPBIS). *See* positive behavioral interventions and supports
Scott, S., 70, 95–96
Scott, T. M., 55
self-concept, 68
self-monitoring, 68
self-regulatory skills, 67–68
self-talk scripts, 74
Seven Keys to a Positive Learning Environment in Your Classroom (Hierck), 22, 46, 62
"Shortage of Farmers," 10
Significant 72 strategy, 25–27, 38, 92
simultaneous interaction, 41–43
Smith, D., 9, 23, 27, 35, 70, 73
Smithgall, C., 2
social behaviors, 67–69, 78
    defined, 67
sociogram of peer relationships, 37–38
Speck, M., 16
standardized tests, 45
STORY strategy, 59
Structure of the Observed Learning Outcome (SOLO) taxonomy, 49–50
student greetings, 27–28, 81
student identity development, 45
student mobility, 28
Sugai, G., 55
survivors, 17–18
sustainability, 4
    alignment to managing learning, 6
systems thinking, 2, 80
    aligning principles to managing learning, 5
    four principles, 4–5
    managing learning element, 1–19, 79
    seven elements, 3–4

T

Tajiri, S., 29
teacher-student relationships, 21–22, 36, 42, 80
    expectations, not rules, 22–25
    strategies for improving, 25–29
teachers
    commitment, 45
    competence, 26, 29
    credibility, 26–27
    enthusiasm, 28–29
    responsibility, 66–67
teaching resilience, 70, 74–75
team building, 38–40, 82
Thomas Jefferson Junior High School (Woodridge, Illinois), 81–97
    background, 82–84
    behavioral management implementation, 84–95
    future work, 95–96
    implementation, 84–85
    office discipline referral data, 84, 87–88, 90, 93–95
    student demographic data, 83
three-to-one praise ratio, 59–60
time management, 32
tissue box theory of student behavior, 65
trust, 26, 29
two-by-ten strategy, 58

U

Unstoppable Learning (Fisher & Frey), 2, 7, 79

V

Vagle, N. D., 31, 34, 39
Varga, M., 26
volition, 68

W

Walker, B., 12
Warnke, J., 82–83
Weber, C., 17, 31, 35, 68, 71, 74, 85–86
Weinstein, C. S., 73
Wiggins, A., 33
Williams, K. C., 13, 27, 35
Win-Win Discipline program, 95–96
Wolcott, G., 59
Woodridge School District 68 (Illinois), 25–27, 38, 59, 81–96
Wright, J., 31

Y

Yet strategy, 60

Unstoppable Learning
Douglas Fisher and Nancy Frey
Discover proven methods to enhance teaching and learning schoolwide. Identify questions educators should ask to guarantee a positive classroom culture where students learn from each other, not just teachers. Explore ways to adapt teaching in response to students' individual needs.
BKF662

Assessing Unstoppable Learning
Tom Hierck and Angela Freese
The Unstoppable Learning model includes seven elements—(1) planning, (2) launching, (3) consolidating, (4) assessing, (5) adapting, (6) managing, and (7) leading. This user-friendly resource focuses on the assessing element, giving readers step-by-step actions for collectively reworking their assessment systems.
BKF735

Adapting Unstoppable Learning
Yazmin Pineda Zapata and Rebecca Brooks
This practical guide expands on the Unstoppable Learning model to explore accessible learning for students with varying needs, from physical disabilities to twice-exceptionality. Forms, tools, and diagrams designed to aid instructional planning are also included.
BKF734

Seven Keys to a Positive Learning Environment in Your Classroom
Tom Hierck
Creating a positive classroom learning environment is a complex but necessary task. By following the seven keys the author outlines, teachers can establish clearer expectations, enhance instruction and assessment practices, and foster quality relationships with students, maximizing the potential of all students.
BKF721

Visit SolutionTree.com or call 800.733.6786 to order.

GL😊BAL PD

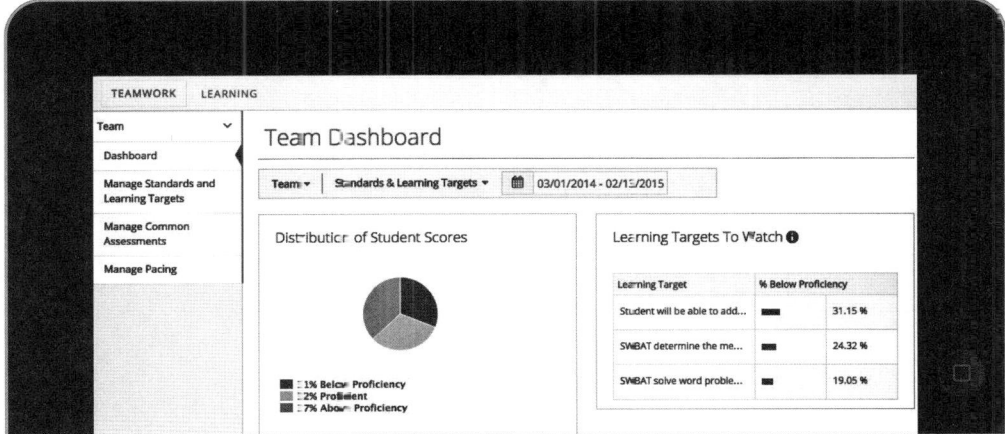

The **Power to Improve** Is in Your Hands

Global PD gives educators focused and goals-oriented training from top experts. You can rely on this innovative online tool to improve instruction in every classroom.

- Get unlimited, on-demand access to guided video and book content from top Solution Tree authors.

- Improve practices with personalized virtual coaching from PLC-certified trainers.

- Customize learning based on skill level and time commitments.

▶ **REQUEST A FREE DEMO TODAY**
SolutionTree.com/GlobalPD

 Solution Tree